796.342

8000272

£ 12.95

D1427407

NORTH EAST INSTITUTE
FARM LODGE
LEARNING CENTRE

Lutz Steinhöfel

Training Exercises for COMPETITIVE TENNIS

Meyer & Meyer Verlag

Original title: Leistungstennis
© 1995 by Meyer & Meyer Verlag, Aachen
Translation: James Beachus, Düsseldorf

Die Deutsche Bibliothek – CIP Einheitsaufnahme

Steinhöfel, Lutz:
Training exercises for competitive tennis / Lutz Steinhöfel.
– Aachen : Meyer und Meyer, 1998
ISBN 3-89124-464-9

All rights reseved. Except for use in a review, the reproduction or utilization
of his work in any electronic, mechanical, or other means, now known or
hereafter invented, including xerography, photocopying and recording, and
in any information retrieval system, is forbidden without the written
permission of publisher.

© 1998 by Meyer & Meyer Verlag, Aachen
Cover photo: Sergi Bruguera, adidas AG, Herzogenaurach
Photos: Düsselpresse Hajo Lange, Neuss-Grefrath:
p. 8, 20, 21, 62, 63, 96, 97, 128, 129, 150, 151
Illustrations: Mischka Kery, Mönchengladbach
Cover Design: Walter J. Neumann, N&N Design-Studio, Aachen
Exposure: typeline, Dagmar Schmitz, Aachen
Lithos: frw, Reiner Wahlen, Aachen
Editorial: Dr. Irmgard Jaeger, Aachen
Printed by Röder + Moll GmbH, Mönchengladbach
Printed in Gemany
ISBN 3-89124-464-9

INDEX

1 Introduction

Certainly in Germany, the home country of the author, the beginning of the boom in tennis was marked by Boris Becker's sensational win at Wimbledon in the mid eighties. Also Steffi Graf's dominance on the international tennis scene, with her numerous wins in the Grand Slam Championships (reaching its zenith in the 1988 Grand Slam), as well as Michael Stich's comet like climb since his win in Wimbledon in 1991, have given this lifetime sport a particular status.

The presence of these three personalities in the top places on the ATP as well as the WTA rank listings and the team successes (Davis Cup – 1988,1989 and 1993; Federation Cup win 1988) all contributed to create a top position in the national and international media of these performances. In particular, increased television coverage, with astronomical viewing quotas for the finals whenever the three German superstars Graf, Becker and Stich were playing, caused the "white" sport to be forced into world-wide professionalisation.

Parallel to this development there was an explosion in the increase of membership in the German Tennis Union as well as an increasing number of qualified coaches and Trainers with a variety of licences ranging from 'C' Trainer (Exercise Leader) to fully qualified German Tennis Trainer Union (abbreviated to 'VDT' in German) Trainers or even Graduate Trainers.

This edition of Training Exercises for Competitive Tennis gives a detailed overview of new selected training exercises and the criteria for setting them up. All are adaptable by not only the experienced tennis trainer but also by trainee and professional coaches at international and national levels.

The palette of over 140 different exercises are not exclusively selected for the competition coach or player – they can also be used in training children, teenagers and lower club qualification classes.

Coaches and trainers seeking innovation and new ideas are able to develop or supplement their own individual teaching programme. Taking into account the five principles for competitive sport (see Hollman/Hettinger 1980), strength, speed, staying power, manoeuvrability and co-ordination, these are the main criteria for training on the tennis court. Many of the exercises include some, and at times all of these five factors, and the notes point to these.

The main task of the coach or trainer is to develop a special rapport with his pupil or group. He must keep an eye on the ability to produce a sensible mixture of hard work and fun on the tennis court.

2 General Criteria for Training

2.1 Warm up and Stretching

At the beginning of each training session there should be a 10-minute obligatory warming up programme containing exercises which prepare the tennis player, both physically and psychologically, for the strains of the training to follow.

The warming up exercise programme will normally start with hopping, side-stepping, backwards running or leg cross-over running preliminary exercises. Following this there is a period of relaxing gymnastic exercises, using the principles of moving from the head to the feet in turn. To increase the heart and blood circulation, improve breathing and increase muscle fibre temperature, the alternatives of 5-10 minutes on the home-trainer exercise bicycle or rope-skipping are both equally suitable and recommended.

A good measure of the adequacy and sufficiency of the warming up phase is when a light sweating effect is reached. The exercise session should be rounded off with stretching exercises – all so often neglected. In this manner one will reach greater body flexibility and elasticity of the moving parts of the skeleton, thus avoiding the danger of injury to the muscles, sinews and joints.

Primarily, the tennis player must ensure that the muscles of the arms, upper body (shoulders, chest and back) as well as the legs (thighs and leg muscles) are warmed up by the training exercises. Similarly, when rounding off the warm up training, on conclusion of the actual tennis training, stretching exercises should also be done in order to guarantee rapid regeneration and recovery from the strains.

The warm up prior to a game, using relaxed ball strokes, is completely opposite to the action-packed rapid hard-hitting in the game for real. The feel for the optimum moment to switch from the slow rate of strike to fluid rapid hitting can only be developed by the individual player.

One can define the initial warm up phase as the psychological tuning process prior to either the training session or tournament match. With the increase of the cardiovascular circulatory rate and breathing and metabolism functions, comes a change in psychological outlook, and this signifies a heightened competitive preparedness in the player.

2.2 Basics and Specialities for Tennis Training

The training 'unit', lasting between at least 60 minutes and a maximum of 120 minutes, is the subject of the illustrated exercises in their basic form, and is the smallest part of the training session. The trainer chooses and feeds in the intensity of the 'unit' according to the time of day when the training period takes place. This calls for a structured arrangement for the medium term training process. The main question the trainer must ask himself is – Is the player or the group/team in the middle of a tournament phase, or running up to one – or is a regeneration or rest period taking place?

**Tomas Carbonell
(Spain)**

Since the athlete, for biological reasons, cannot always be on top form, and because the structure of training and its content have to change periodically to take into account the gradual development of athletic performance, the principle of period phasing (Jonath 1988, 215) has to be introduced.

The European player's tournament cycle contains, for example, the indoor and the open-air seasons or the national team championships (Bundesliga). Generally, in this last phase, training is concentrated and no account is made for any particular conditioning aspects. On the contrary, in the preparatory training phase, technique and conditioning elements can be incorporated into the open-air sessions in March/April when this takes place.

During the regeneration or rest periods, after the open-air season, or prior to the tournament season, a relatively lengthy (4-6 weeks) period of condition training (aerobic stamina and speed training) as well as technique training can be added to the training programme. The international tournament calendar (ATP and WTA) is such that a free period of this kind is almost only possible in December, just before the New Zealand and Australian tournament series.

The ATP and WTA calendar event dates, together with the application of the current computerised systems, do not allow the player in the high international categories (Top 200), who is seeking to improve his rank placing, any possibility to employ the period phasing principle. This is unlike swimmers or track athletes who experience two or three seasonal highpoints.

One possibility to permit a training plan over a longer period can be seen in connection with the German National Men's Team Championship (Bundesliga), which takes place in one block in the months of August and September. This allows the trainer to construct a steady time build-up with limited period phasing, thus giving an organised training and match cycle.

However, for the German tennis protégés facing the international tournament scene, the opportunity to incorporate such a sensible medium term periodical build-up to training, is almost illusionary. On the one hand the computer pressurises the player to defend the previous year's points, while, on the other hand, he avoids dropping rank placing by striving to win at all costs in qualifying, challenger or satellite tournaments.

The classical periodic training build-up for youths is therefore practically only possible in certain circumstances. Certainly as far as condition training is concerned, the physical basic elements of strength, mobility (stamina, speed and staying power) and gymnastics have to be built-up during the specific time-frame of the winter indoor season when fewer tournaments are taking place.

It is the trainer's responsibility to determine the rate of training intensity. After a systematic warming up programme, including stretching (see 2.1), training exercises must be conceived such that the rate of increase from the simple to the complex exercises is undertaken in a sensible manner. Exercises specialising on match performance and service return should come at the end of the 60-120 minute training session. Specifically, intense tennis condition training (see Exercise examples in Section 'C' later) should round the training off and not take place at the beginning.

The training examples illustrated later in this book are divided into four categories:

Singles Training   – S 1 to S 20
Group Training   – G 1 to G 31
Doubles Training – D 1 to D 10
Condition Training – C 1 to C 11

2.3 Singles Training

Singles training allows the trainer to concentrate considerably more on the individual. Technical and tactical points can be addressed, played through and studied in great detail. In the timeframe of between 45 to 90 minutes for each training 'unit' (singles training hour), the learning process of important elementary strokes and their assimilation and improvement is made more effective. For example the teaching of the attacking back-hand stroke demands a number of individual and combined exercises over a long period.

Generally it should be noted, that not only should weaknesses be corrected, but also inherent strengths of the player should be spotted and encouraged. The trainer's ability to observe and identify all these points in his pupil is the absolute basis for the production of a constructive training programme. The coach must also be able to draw from his own competition experiences on the tournament court.

Unlike group training, singles training brings with it the opportunity for thorough and individual discussion of singles training points. This is the only way during training for the tennis coach to be able to go over the problems of technical weaknesses and eventually match situations or motivation aspects.

2.4 Group and Team Training

On the other side of the coin, group training, with two, three or four players means more complicated exercises with a greater requirement for combination than the singles training. Thus, correction of individual mistakes takes on a lower priority. Stroke play, generally, between all pupils in the group or team, should be as dynamic and varied as possible. Each player should have as few inactive periods as possible and should stay constantly on the move. The change round of positions during the training exercises can be differentiated so that each player is given a variety of actions in rotation – for example this can range from a baseline position with a lot of activity, to the net position with less intense activity. For repetitive stroke exercise, a pause is recommended after four or five shots – similar to match play – whilst the next player waits his turn.

The important element of group training is the harmony and the motivation of the players amongst themselves. Players of similar strength can measure themselves against their partners, and accordingly improve their own competitiveness. This factor is the optimum challenge in training, and while care must be taken to avoid any over- or under-reaction, it constitutes the best possible work-out for the group or team training session.

The tennis coach faces a particular challenge when training the tennis team (which in Germany consists of six players), not only for the top category levels, but also when training amateur team groups. Individuals have to be melted into a team, and this is just as applicable whether one is dealing with an amateur class or training at national level – even a Davis Cup team can prove to be a challenge! Psychological aspects play a large role in the relationship coach – player.

Training, with 4–6 players calls for a mixture of singles and group training principles. Whenever possible, training can take place on more than one court – ideally parallel. The trainer will use the rotation principle to move the players round the various positions at regular intervals. This calls for a coach who possesses organisational talent, ability to create a good overview, experience, a keen eye, spontaneity and understanding.

Placing a player in the youth class into a men's training session can produce both a challenge and stimulus, assuming the youth has the appropriate physical, mental and technical attributes.

Further optimisation and individualisation of the training for the higher grade classes can be best achieved with the use of an assistant. A mutual under-standing and exact knowledge of the performance level of the team and its members are absolute prerequisites for fruitful co-operation and confidence-building of the trainer and co-trainer.

2.5 Training for Doubles

In the training exercises later in this book, the tasks D 1 – D 10 are exclusively devoted to exercises for doubles training. They are particularly designed for couples who have played together already. Mutual understanding, harmony and synchronised thinking are the main overriding criteria for the doubles team. It is up to the trainer to target problems of synchronised thinking between the players (for example – failure to cover the middle court), and correct these.

The main aim of every doubles training session is to practice the elementary principle doubles strokes – the service, return and volley. Training is only effective if it is carried out under the conditions likely to be experienced in a match situation. Items such as the defensive position and getting out of precarious situations should be practised and talked through. Each player must be given the chance in training of playing from his strongest side, while not denying the question of trying out a change to the weaker side to be brought into the session. Perhaps the most important point regarding doubles is that partners must possess the temperament to be able to get along with each other and read each others' thoughts.

The characteristics of each of the doubles partners can be quite opposite to each other. Take, for instance, the offensive server and volley player in contrast with the fine stroke player. There are some world class players who prove this point – Woodforde/Woodbridge (Australia), Casal/Sanchez (Spain) or Eltingh/Haarhuis (Netherlands) are all well versed doubles combinations who have achieved optimum harmonisation with each other. The attacking hard-hitting type complements the more defensive fine stroke player, and vice versa.

2.6 Condition Training

Exercises shown in the book as C 1-C 11 are designed as exercises which take place at the end of the training 'unit'. Dependent on the seasonal period when the training takes place – normal training or during the tournament season – condition training in the form of sprints and spurts on the tennis court can take up to 20-30 minutes.

The intensity of this form of training also is dependent on the overall training programme i.e. whether one is the preparation, regenerative or rest period. Daily training usually makes use of the integration and combination of two exercises. On the last day before a match, intensive sprinting etc., should be avoided.

After intensive sprint training, using the length of the tennis court, one should use jogging to round the session off and finish with stretching and several gymnastic exercises. The spectrum illustrated in the series C 1-C 11 serves also as an addition for singles and group training.

One of the main criteria for the trainer is the suitability of exercises on the tennis court. Training sessions extending beyond these – stamina and staying power – can take place in woods or on the athletics track away from the court.

3 The task of the Tennis Trainer and Exercise Leader

In Germany, and generally in Europe, the professional Trainer or Exercise Leader often has a varied spectrum of tasks to fulfil in a tennis club. The main elements of his tasks are the recognition of talent in pupils at a young age and the coaching of various age groups of boys and girls in either singles, groups or in teams. At best he will change a talented child into a national, or even better, an international top-class player.

The principle characteristics of the trainer are the ability to make critical observations, the determination to achieve results, psychological insight, a balanced sense of feel as well as an affinity towards educational and teaching applications.

Prerequisites for an effective lesson on the tennis court, are organisational capability, spontaneity, idealism, flexibility when faced with disturbances, and in particular good technical ability in order to be able to demonstrate the various shots (e.g., drive, slice and topspin) in detail. When teaching it is important to possess an eye for each individual part of the movement in order to be able to give the right advice for correction of a fault. The coach must also be able to serve up practice balls with precision to his pupils, as well as be able to cover and place return shots, in all variations – soft or hard, short or long, and with varying speeds. A good sense of timing for stroke play – stemming from the coach's own experience – is absolutely an essential part of competitive training.

Besides correcting technical faults, the coach must not overlook the tactical side of match play with regard to tips and assessment of a potential opponent – whether he or she is an attacking or a defensive player. To this end the coach will have to simulate match situations, or, talk through the tactical possibilities in match training sessions.

For the qualified coach, the correct amount of theoretical knowledge and practical ability are usually inherently combined. The coach's long years of tournament experience, at national and international levels, must somehow be transmitted to the pupil. However this does not replace the optimum of training.

Training must still be complemented with elements of teaching such as psychological (praise and motivation), educational talent and didactic elements. On the other hand a complete tennis theorist, without any great degree of tournament experience, can still be an excellent coach and trainer.

Similarly an inborn feeling for the appropriate degree of intensity of training is also an essential ability. An over- or understatement of the training intensity should be avoided both in singles and group sessions. Here – content and intensity – all lie in the hands of the coach.

The sports teacher in general, and particularly the tennis coach is a person who creates respect for him- or herself, and is a mentor, a coach, friend and even, in part, a father figure, all in one. The long-term responsibility for the upbringing of young persons in such an important part of their life, lies in the hands of the person entrusted to deliver the measures – the coach.

The areas for which a coach is responsible in a club are often extremely varied. He is responsible for the training of children, young people and grown-ups. The training programme, including the role played by one or more assistants, is only fully organised when individual training and training for groups of two, three or four players as well as team training, have been efficiently locked into an overall strategic plan.

The factor of time is the basis of every training session. A training 'unit' or 'hour' lasts 40 to 60 minutes, and, exceptionally as long as 90 minutes. For group or team training one should allow for at least one and a half to two hours, excluding the warm-up, gymnastics and post training stretching exercises. One must carefully consider how many people should be trained at once.

Ball quality and the supply of them is an important point – one should allow for at least 60-100 balls being available. Additionally, training aids must be thought of for each session – these can range from baskets, tennis ball canisters for use as targets during certain training exercises, to video-cameras and the like.

For both the coach and the pupil, optimum conditions should be the watchword to create effective training – in general, poor material is a false saving.

A good racket, with properly tensioned gut-strings, appropriate clothing and comfortable shoes all make the basis for solid training.

In many clubs in Germany there is an honorary committee which oversees and co-ordinates the organisation of the sport. In such a case the trainer, on the one hand, acts as the go-between for the club leadership and player cadre, and, on the other hand he has a role as go-between for the club and authorities – county, union and national authorities. Thus the responsibility for the sporting prowess lies principally in the coach's hands.

How good the group listings for the team, or the ranking of individuals turn out, is the direct product of the training and the long-term build-up by the tennis coach and his team.

The club executives work together with the coach to produce a target orientated financial plan, set to deliver either the broad interest in the sport, or achieve a place in the competitive scene. The transition from the youth classes into the adult class should flow naturally following these organisational ground rules.

4 Training for Competitive Tennis

Almost all the illustrated training exercises (in this book) are designed with competitive tennis in mind, and build up to an automated series of techniques. Nevertheless, with one or two minor exceptions, they can be used equally as well at lower technical levels.

The position of the coach or trainer is indicated by the letter 'T', while the players are marked as 'a', 'b' or 'c'. Practically all the exercises for singles can be used with two or three players on the court without any problem. See for example Exercises 'S 12' or 'S 14'. Similarly many of the group exercises can be used, in a reduced format, and applied to singles training. Examples are 'G 6' or 'G 7'.

A combination of the illustrated exercises can be sensibly applied to team training on more than one court and with up to six players. While the coach can only be in one place, he can delegate particular tasks to an assistant on a parallel court. Condition training exercises always belong at the end of the training session!

In the training for upper league classes, the coach must be able to play actively with the pupils. In order to heighten the interest and create a dynamic training session, the coach should be in a position to place himself in the role of a sparring partner. The decision to do this lies in the hands of the coach, however this role is not always absolutely necessary. The integration of the coach in play brings with it variety and motivation, as each pupil feels himself intensively and effectively challenged. The position of the coach can be also taken by one of the pupils quite effectively. In such cases then the coach observes and assumes the role of discussion leader.

The Performance Relevant Parameters of the Illustrated Exercises are:

> Training Aims
> Training Intensity
> Length of Training (Time)

All the exercises are listed with at least one variation – see Chapter 5.3. Variations of the Training Exercises, and are supplemented with notes – see Chapter 5.4 Notes.

4.1 Training Aims

Each training 'hour' and each exercise must have an aim. The aim of an individual training session is the systematic work on the groundstrokes (forehand, backhand), with variations of the techniques – drive, topspin or slice. In addition to these there is also basic training of the groundstrokes – volley, smash and service. Correction and improvement of the various special strokes such as drop shot, drop volley, the lob, topspin lob, the attacking stroke and passing shot, as well as the variations of the second service (kick, twist or slice service) – all contribute to the broad spectrum of the training aims.

Very often groundstrokes will be combined with the special strokes, for example, depending on the situation, a two-handed or single handed backhand slice, both in singles and group training.

During a 60-minute training session the coach will be able to play through approximately five training exercises, each lasting about 8-10 minutes. Which exercises are chosen for this, will depend on the training aim for the session.

As an example the long-term work-out of the attacking stroke (backhand slice) or the twist service, demands repetitive and varied practice until the stroke comes automatically. The technical detailed work should be carried out separately to the combined training exercises (see 'S 8' and 'S 12'). The relevant parameters for the stroke are percentage play, precision, power-play, leg-work, mobility, balance, reaction and any match simulation being used in the exercise.

4.2 Training Intensity

A compromise between intensity of training and diversion is very important. The intensity applied in training is very dependent on the condition and disposition of the pupil. The basis of every training session is to begin with a rhythm and stroke training session (see 'S 1', 'S 2' and 'S 3'). This can be followed by intensive drill exercises with frequent rally exchanges and footwork practice (see 'S 13' and 'S 16').

The measurement for the training intensity grades of low, medium, medium-high or high is subjective, and can be increased or slowed down according to the coach's judgement. This can be regulated according to the pauses which follow an exchange of strokes or the gap between sessions.

In general, breaks in training will be controlled by the coach. The strain created by training set too high – overtraining – can lead both to a reduction in the performance effectiveness and to symptoms of sickness and injury (Roethig 1977).

4.3 Length of Training (Time)

A further regulatory factor for all training exercises is the recommended length of training, which normally lasts between 5-10 minutes. To achieve a high intensity grade, the exercise time should be shortened (see 'S 17' or 'G 16'). Vice versa, the timing can be lengthened up to 15 minutes (see 'G 13 or 'G 21').

Using the rotation method in group training, the length of training time for each player will last approximately five minutes. In a lower training intensity factor (aerobic exercises), for example in the training of groundstroke play without much movement, the length of the exercise session can be easily extended.

Exercises with repetition of the passing ball stroke can reach into the anaerobic lactated regions if carried out in series. In such cases the illustrated timing must be adhered to. Again in general, the length of training time lies in the hands and judgement of the coach.

5. Training Exercises – Practical

5.1 Diagram Explanations (Legend)

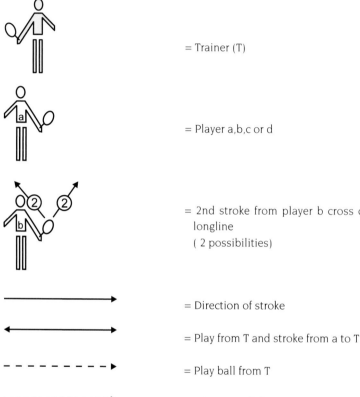

= Trainer (T)

= Player a,b,c or d

= 2nd stroke from player b cross court or longline
(2 possibilities)

= Direction of stroke

= Play from T and stroke from a to T

= Play ball from T

= Direction of player's movement

= Lob

= Ball strike

= Ball strike in the marked area (Target area)

= 1st stroke from a

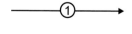

= 1st stroke from T

5.2 Abbreviations

a,b,c,d	=	Player a through to Player d
A	=	Attacking ball
CR	=	Cross (diagonal)
LL	=	Longline ball
P	=	Passing shot
BH	=	Backhand
BH-S	=	Backhand smash
S	=	Smash
SL	=	Slice (Stroke with back spin)
T	=	Trainer
TSP	=	Top spin (Stroke with forward spin)
TSP-LOB	=	Top spin lob
V	=	Volley
FH	=	Forehand
FH/CC/BH	=	Forehand cross court from the backhand corner
FH/CC/S	=	Forehand into the cross court (Short)
FH/TSP/V	=	Forehand top spin volley
V-Stop	=	Drop volley
Winner	=	Groundstroke (risk shot, played at speed)

5.3 Variations for the Training Exercises

Each training exercise offers several different variation possibilities. There is no limit to the trainer's ingenuity in this respect. He is able to decide whether the exercises are reduced or enlarged.

The position of the Trainer (T) on the court is important for forehand or backhand corners, or at the net. In this way the desired cross or longline strokes by the players (a,b or c) are determined. In addition the rate of practice can be varied by changing the way in which the feed balls or the targeting of the trainer's returns in the course of the exercise are made. The trainer can control the speed of the ball by either accelerating or slowing down the return shots he plays. Even with varying player strengths within a group, the trainer can determine the various possible situations by introducing changes such as the long slow ball, hardness of play, height, direction and spin (slice or top spin).

All the illustrated exercises and explanations are set up for a right-handed player. When a left-handed player is present it is necessary to switch the thought process regarding the feed ball service and the targeted return. See exercise 'G 21'.

Goran Ivanisevic
(Croatia)

5.4 Notes

The notes, which are included with each of the training exercises, give the trainer tips regarding the aims and basic factors to be taken into consideration when using the exercise. For example – percentage shots and precision of the groundstrokes.

The important points as well as the time recommendations (timing of an exercise within the training session) are laid down. In addition to this the trainer gets an aid in determining the speed, length and height of the return shot that he should play. For particularly intensive exercises, the trainer will be able to note the necessary recovery rest breaks he should apply with respect to the length (time) of the training. From the player's viewpoint, the notes give the characteristics of each of the exercises.

Niki Pilic and Martin Sinner (Germany)

S Singles Training (S 1)

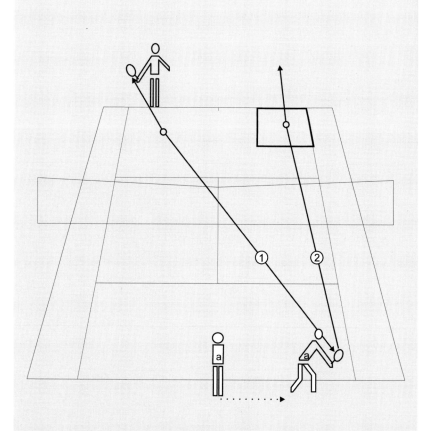

S 1 Groundstrokes

T: Feed (from the FH corner)
      Feed 1 + 2 into the FH corner

a: 1   = FH-CR
      2   = FH-LL-Winner

Aim: Groundstrokes (percentage shot, rhythm)

Intensity: Medium

Time: Approx 5 minutes

1. Variation:
a: 1   = BH-CR
      2   = BH-LL-Winner

2. Variation:
a: 1   = FH/CC/BH
      2   = FH-LL-Winner

3. Variation:
a: 1   = FH/CC/BH
      2   = BH-CR to T
      3   = FH-LL-Winner

4. Variation:
T: Feed from the net

Notes:
Basic exercise for use at the beginning of a training session. Groundstroke precision, rhythm practice, change of pace, concentration on the stroke (strengths and weaknesses).

S Singles Training (S 2)

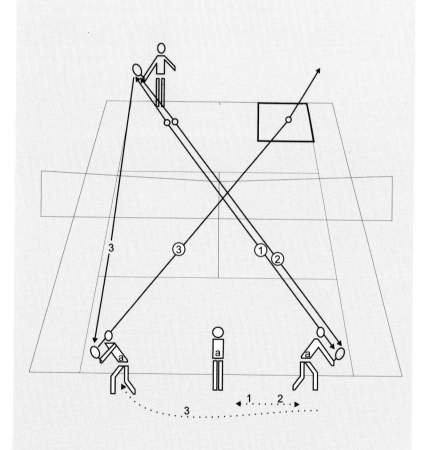

S 2 Groundstrokes

T: Feed (from the FH corner)
    1 + 2 = into the FH corner
    3   = into the BH corner

a: 1 + 2 = FH-CR
    3   = BH-CR-Winner (into the marked target area)

Aim: Groundstrokes (percentage, precision, change of pace)

Intensity: Medium-high

Time: Approx 5 minutes

1. Variation:
T: Feed from the BH corner

a: 1 + 2 = BH-CR
    3   = FH-CR-Winner

2. Variation:
T: Feed from the BH corner

a: 1 + 2 = FH/CC/BH
    3   = FH-CR-Winner

3. Variation:
T: Feed from the net

Notes:
Percentage and precision of groundstrokes, rhythm training on the move;
application of frequency lies in the trainer's hands; player uses various stroke
speeds (groundstroke rather than winner)!

S | Singles Training (S 3)

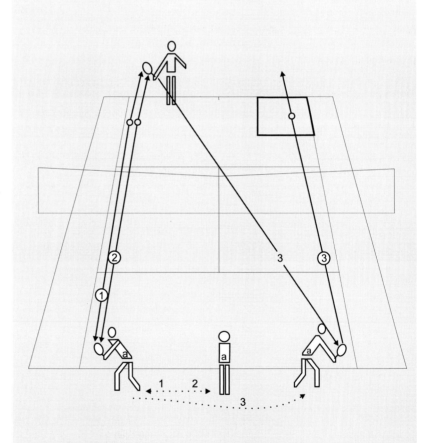

S 3 Groundstrokes

T: Feed (from the FH corner)
       1 + 2 = into the BH corner
       3   = into the FH corner

a: 1 + 2 = BH-LL
       3   = FH-LL-Winner (into target area)

Aim: Groundstrokes (percentage, precision, change of pace)

Intensity: Medium-high

Time: Approx 5 minutes

1.   Variation:
T: Feed from the BH corner
       1 + 2 = Feed into FH corner
       3   = Feed into BH corner

a: 1 + 2 = FH-LL
       3   = BH-LL-Winner

2.   Variation:
T: Feed from the net

Notes:
Exercise for the beginning of training; percentage and precision of groundstrokes;
change of pace using various speeds in returning the groundstroke and winner!

S Singles Training (S 4)

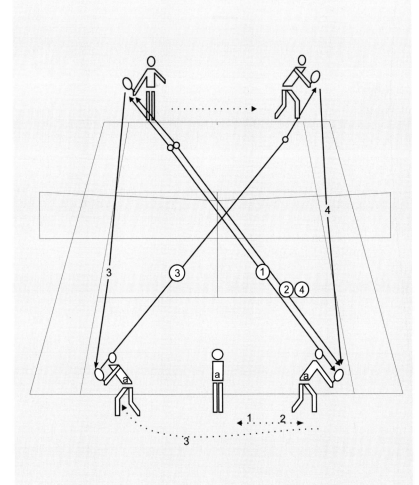

S 4 Groundstrokes

T: 1 + 2 = Feed (into the FH corner)
    3   = Feed LL into the BH corner
    4   = Feed LL into the FH corner
         (T follows up !)

a: 1 + 2 = FH-CR
    3   = BH-CR
    4 + 5 = FH-CR
         etc.

Aim: Groundstrokes (percentage, precision, rhythm)

Intensity: Medium-high

Time: Approx 5 minutes

1. Variation:
T: 1 + 2 = Feed into BH corner
    3   = Feed LL into FH corner
    4   = Feed LL into BH corner
         (T follows up !)

a: 1 + 2 = BH-CR
    3   = FH-CR
    4 + 5 = BH-CR
         etc.

Notes:
Rhythm exercise for the beginning of training; controlled speed. Player gets used to running and stroke rhythm: The exercise can also be used for group training ('b' takes up the position and movements of 'T').

S Singles Training (S 5)

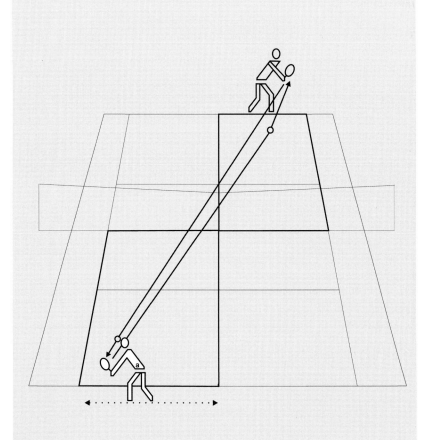

S 5 Groundstrokes

T: BH-CR
a: BH-CR (for points – only in the outlined field)

Aim: Groundstrokes – as in a competition (percentage, precision)

Intensity: Medium

Time: Approx 5-10 minutes each side

1.   Variation:
T: FH-CR
a: FH-CR

2.   Variation:
T: FH-LL
a: BH-LL

3.   Variation:
T: BH-LL
a: FH-LL

4.   Variation:
T: BH-CR
a: FH/CC/BH

5.   Variation:
T: FH/CC/BH
a: FH/CC/BH

Notes:
Basic exercise after a long training pause; percentage in playing groundstrokes;
concentration on playing the stroke (strength/weakness)!

S — Singles Training (S 6)

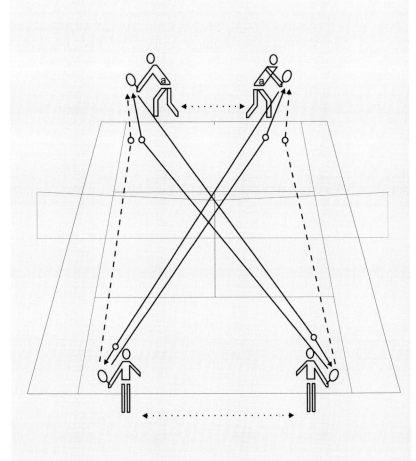

6 Groundstrokes

T: 1 + 2   = Feed FH-CR
    3 + 4 + 5 = FH-LL
    6   = BH-CR
    7 + 8   = BH-LL
          (T follows up)
          etc.

a: 1 + 2 = FH-CR
    3 + 4 = BH-LL
    5 + 6 = BH-CR
    7 + 8 = FH-LL
        etc.

Aim: Percentage, precision of the groundstroke

Intensity: Medium-high

Time: Approx 5-8 minutes

Notes:
Optimum exercise for getting one's eye in; all the groundstrokes can be comfortably played through on the move. The trainer, who moves with the play, observes player's leg work and technique; ability to concentrate.

S · Singles Training (S 7)

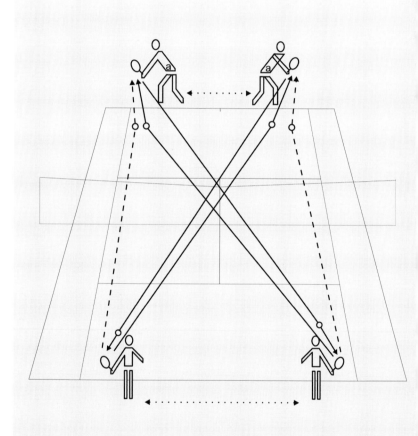

S 7 Groundstrokes

T: Feed FH-CR or BH-CR
(T changes from FH-CR to BH-CR at will)

a: FH-CR or BH-CR

Aim: Rhythm and percentage of the groundstroke

Intensity: Medium-high

Time: Approx 5-8 minutes

Variation:
T: Feed FH-LL or BH-LL
(T changes from FH-LL to BH-LL at will)

a: FH-LL or BH-LL

Notes:
Exercise to get the eye attuned, which concentrates the mind of the player; rhythm and precision in groundstroke play are the main aims of the exercise. For the variations (LL), play as close as possible to the sidelines! The exercise can be carried out with two players (exercise with point play as in a competition).

35

S Singles Training (S 8)

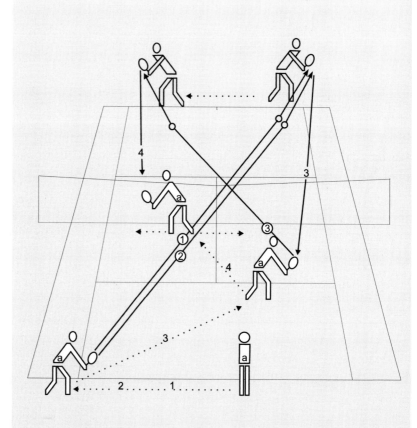

S 8 Groundstrokes

T: 1 + 2 = Feed into BH corner
   3   = Into the FH corner (on the T-line)
   4   = Passing shot and play out the point
          (T follows up)

a: 1 + 2 = FH/CC/BH (run round the BH)
   3   = FH-A-CR
   4   = V and play out the point with T

Aim: Running round the backhand
           Attacking ball
           Volley
           Mobility
           Leg work

Intensity: High

Time: Approx 5 minutes

1.   **Variation:**
a: 1   = FH/CC/BH (running round the backhand)
    2   = BH-CR
    3   = BH-A-LL
    4   = V
          and play out the point (T following up)

2.   **Variation:**
a: 1 + 2 = FH-CR
    3   = BH-A-LL
    4   = V and play out the point

Notes
Combined exercise under attack conditions; leg work practice (running round
the backhand), covering the whole court; timing between baseline and net.

S   Singles Training (S 9)

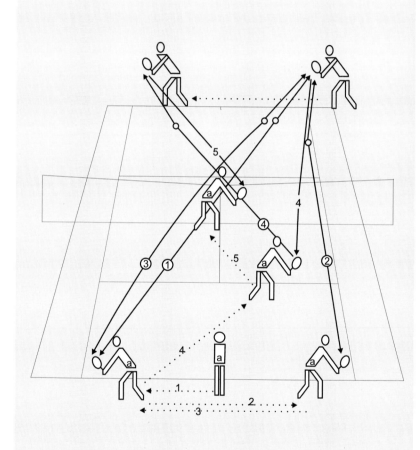

S 9 Groundstrokes

T: Feed from the baseline (BH side)
      Feed up 4 balls + passing shot (LL or CR)
      (T follows up)

a: 1   = BH-SL-CR
      2   = FH-LL
      3   = BH-TSP-CR
      4   = FH-A-CR
      5   = V
               and play out the point

Aim: Backhand variations
            Attacking ball play
            Volley
            Timing

Intensity: High

Time: 5-10 minutes

1.   Variation:
a: 1   = BH-SL-LL
      2   = FH-CR
      3   = BH-TSP-LL
      4   = FH-A-CR
      5   = V
               and play out the point

2.   Variation:
a: BH varied at will (TSP or SL)

Notes:
Complex, match simulating exercise; covering the whole court. Variation possibilities for backhand play; trainer can be replaced by a second player ('b'). An exact feed must be served up by trainer (low ball feed from trainer = TSP and high feed from trainer = SL)!

S Singles Training (S 10)

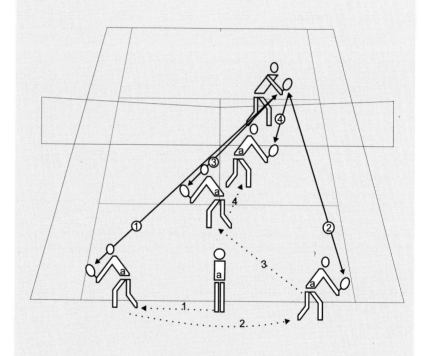

S 10   Groundstrokes / Attacking Ball / Volley

T: Feed from the net (BH side)

a: 1   = BH-CR
    2   = FH-LL
    3   = BH-A-CR
    4   = V-Duel out with T

Aim: Groundstrokes (percentage, power-play)

Intensity: High

Time: Approx 5-8 minutes

Variation:
T: Feed from the net (FH side)

a: 1   = FH-CR
    2   = BH-LL
    3   = FH-A-CR
    4   = V-Duel out with T

Notes:
Transition from safe, forceful groundstrokes to the volley played on the move forward; practice reaction in playing the volley; T replaceable with a 2nd player. Trainer must be able to play precision volleying.

41

S SINGLES TRAINING (S 11)

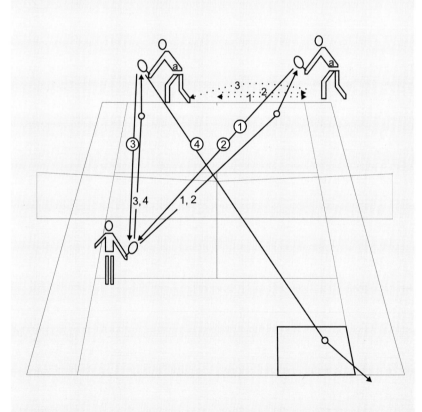

S 11   Forehand

T: Feed from the net (BH side)

a: 1 + 2 = FH/CC/BH to T (run round the backhand)
3   = FH-LL to T
4   = FH-CR-Winner (into target area)

Aim: Forehand (power-play stroke)
Mobility (leg work)
Timing

Intensity: High

Time: Approx 5 minutes

Variation:
T: Feed from the net (FH side)

a: 1 + 2 = FH-LL (run round the backhand)
3   = FH-CR
4   = FH-LL-Winner

Notes:
Special exercise for playing the forehand, particularly suited for clay courts (also possible on fast courts!), improvement of speed and mobility; T must vary feed serves from the baseline (feed ball No 4 into the T-line area !).

S SINGLES TRAINING (S 12)

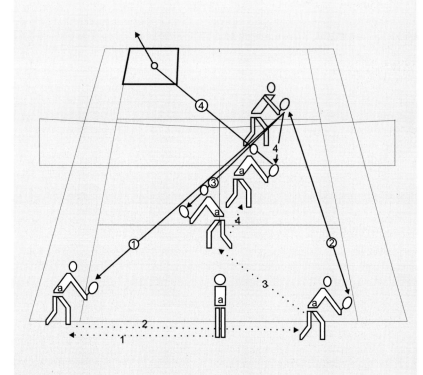

S 12   Forehand / Attacking Ball / Volley

T: Feed 1-4 from the net (BH side)

a: 1   = FH/CC/BH
      2   = FH-LL
      3   = BH-A-CR
      4   = FH-TSP-V(into target area)

Aim: Forehand (power-play stroke)
            Attacking Ball
            Special stroke (top spin volley)

Intensity: High

Time: Approx 5 minutes

Variation:

T: Feed 1-4 from the net (FH side)

a: 1   = FH-CR
      2   = FH-LL (run round the BH)
      3   = FH-A-CR
      4   = FH-TSP-V into BH corner

Notes:
Special exercise for playing the forehand, leg work, mobility, timing in the
transition from groundstroke to volley; top spin volley requires ability for
correct anticipation and technique – watch for racket grip hold on the volley.

S SINGLES TRAINING (S 13)

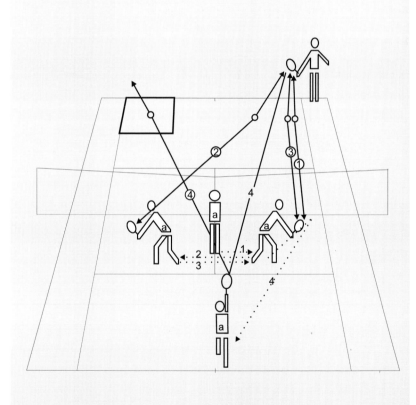

S 13   Volley / Smash

T: Feed from the baseline (BH side)

a: 1   = FH-V-LL
      2   = BH-V-CR
      3   = FH-V-LL + touch the net
      4   = S-CR (from the jump) into the target area

Aim: Volley (precision, power-play, percentage)

Intensity: Medium-high

Time: Approx 5 minutes

Variation:
T: Feed from the baseline (FH side)

a: 1   = BH-V-LL
      2   = FH-V-CR
      3   = BH-V-LL + touch the net
      4   = S-LL from the jump

Notes:
Mobility and leg work playing the volley and smash shots. Trainer decides the rate of play by his feed serves (particularly for the smash shot), player must move in all directions.

S SINGLES TRAINING (S 14)

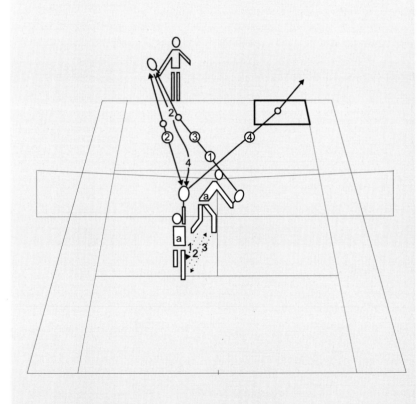

S 14   Volley / Smash

T: Feed from the baseline (FH side)

a: 1   = V to T
    2   = S to T
    3   = V to T
    4   = S into BH corner (in the target area)

Aim: Volley (percentage, power-play)
       Smash shot (power-play, precision)
       Leg work

Intensity: High

Time: Approx 5 minutes

1.   Variation:
T: Feed from the baseline (BH side)

a: 1   = Lower V to T
    2   = S to T
    3   = Lower V to T
    4   = S into the FH corner

2.   Variation:
T: Feed from the baseline (BH side)

a: 1   = V to T
    2   = S to T
    3   = V-Stop
    4   = BH-S-LL

Notes:
Mobility and leg work playing the volley and smash shots. The length and precision of the volley is important. Trainer must exercise timing and sensibility when serving up the feeds.

S   Singles Training (S 15)

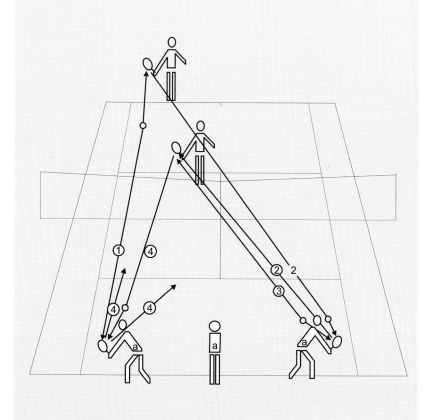

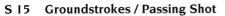

S 15   Groundstrokes / Passing Shot

T: Feed from the baseline (FH side)
1 - 3 = Groundstrokes – direction at will
4   = Attacking shot (either A or V)
5   = V and play out the point
       (T follows up)

a: 1 - 3 = Groundstrokes to T into the FH corner
4   = P-CR or P-LL
5   = Play out the point

Aim: Groundstrokes (percentage, length)
Passing shot (match simulated)

Intensity: High

Time: Approx 10 minutes

Variation:
T: Feed from the baseline (BH side)
1 - 3 = Groundstrokes - direction at will
4   = A or V
5   = V and play out the point
       (T follows up)

a: 1 - 3 = Groundstrokes to T into the BH corner
4   = P-CR or P-LL
5   = Play out the point

Notes:
Match simulated exercise; player must free himself from a defensive position.
Passing shot to be played as in a match. Requires a high degree of accuracy
from the trainer (safe feed, attacking ball and volley). Trainer replaceable by a
2nd player.

S   Singles Training (S 16)

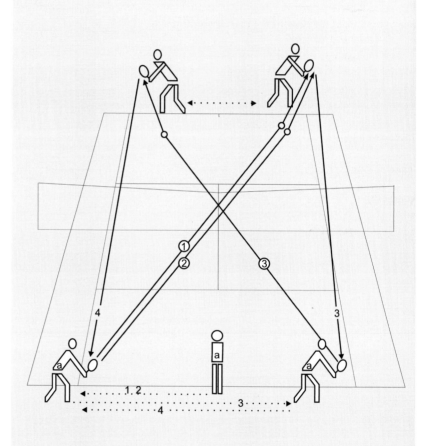

S 16   Groundstrokes

T: 1 + 2 = BH-CR
   3   = BH-LL
   4   = FH-LL
       (T follows up)
   5   = same as 1+2 etc.

a: 1 + 2 = FH/CC/BH (from the BH corner)
   3   = FH-CR
   4   = BH-LL
   5 + 6 = same as 1+2 etc.

Aim: Groundstrokes (percentage, precision, length)

Intensity: High

Time: Approx 5 minutes

Variation:
T: 1 + 2 = FH-CR
   3   = FH-LL
   4   = BH-LL
       (T follows up)
   5 + 6 = same as 1+2 etc.

a: 1 + 2 = FH-CR
   3   = BH-CR
   4   = FH-LL
   5 + 6 = same as 1+2 etc.

Notes:
Exercise also possible for a 2nd player; percentage and precision of ground-strokes. Leg work (running round the BH – places large demands on the trainer; rate of play!)

53

S Singles Training (S 17)

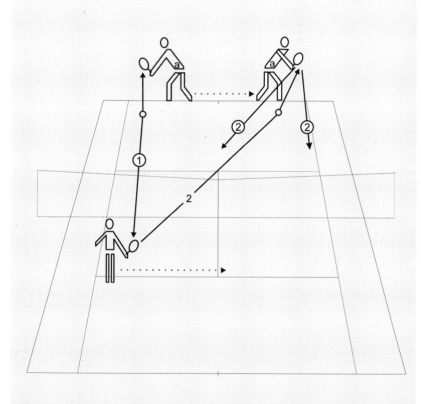

S 17   Passing Ball Shot

T: 1   = Feed into the FH corner (from net/BH side)
   2   = V-CR into the BH corner

a: 1   = FH-LL to T
   2   = P-BH-CR or P-BH-LL

Aim: Passing ball shot (match play simulation)

Intensity: Medium-high

Time: Approx 3-5 minutes per session

1.   Variation:
T: 1   = Feed into the BH corner (from net/BH side)
   2   = V into the FH corner and play out the point

a: 1   = BH-CR to T
   2   = P-FH-CR or P-FH-LL and play out the point

2.   Variation:
T: 1   = Feed into the BH corner (from net/FH side)
   2   = V into the FH corner and play out the point

a: 1   = BH-LL to T
   2   = P-FH-CR or P-FH-LL and play out the point

3.   Variation:
T: 1   = Feed into the FH corner (from net/FH side)
   2   = V into the BH corner and play out the point

a: 1   = FH-CR to T
   2   = P-BH-CR or P-BH-LL and play out the point

Notes:
Passing ball shot on the move, leg work, sensing the position of the opponent (represented by T or 2nd player). Lob as variation to passing shot; exercise also possible with a 2nd player instead of T. It is not essential that the point is played out on each occasion! Ensure that the recovery rest breaks are taken !

S Singles Training (S 18)

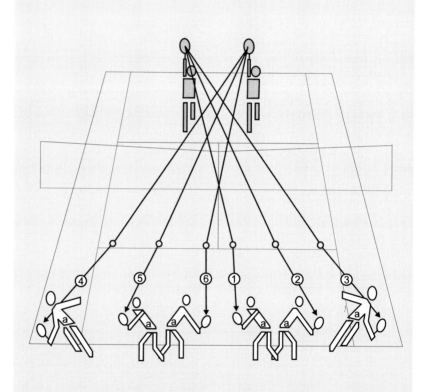

S 18   The return

T: Service (from the T-line – deuce side)
   1   = Serve onto Player a's BH
   2   = Serve onto Player a's body
   3   = Serve onto Player a's FH
      Service (from the T-line – advantage side)
   4   = Serve onto Player a's BH
   5   = Serve onto Player a's body
   6   = Serve onto Player a's FH

Aim: Return shot (technique, reaction)

Intensity: Low

Time: Approx 10-15 minutes

1.   Variation:
Service from T-line without indicating direction beforehand

2.   Variation:
2nd service by T as twist or slice

Notes:
Exercising the return shot in isolation; technique (blocking the return on the move forward), reaction training. Match preparation against a good server.

S — Singles Training (S 19)

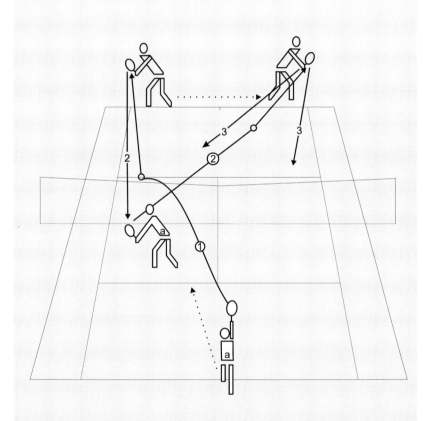

S 19   Service / Volley

a: 1   = Service CR (1st and 2nd Service)
   2   = V into T's BH corner
   3   = V
       and play out the point

T: 2   = RETURN-LL
   3   = P-CR or P-LL
       and play out the point

Aim: Service (precision, power-play)

Intensity: Medium-high

Time: Approx 10 minutes

1.   Variation:

a: 1   = Service onto T's BH (1st and 2nd Service)
   2   = V-CR
       and play out the point

T: 2   = RETURN-CR
   3   = P or Lob

2.   Variation:

a: 1   = Any service
   2   = V into either of T's corners
   3   = Play out the point

T: 2   = RETURN
   3   = P-CR or P-LL
       and play out the point

Notes:
Transition from service to volley (leg work), mobility when volleying, covering the court whilst at the net. Possible to replace trainer with 2nd player; places demand on the trainer for a quick lower return.

S Singles Training (S 20)

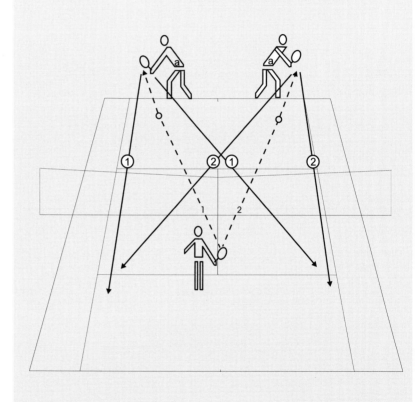

S 20   Passing Shot

T: Feed 1 into the FH corner
     Feed 2 into the BH corner

a: 1   = FH-P
     2   = BH-P on the run

Aim: Leg work
           Sprinting on the turn
           Co-ordination

Intensity: High

Time: One series of 6 balls within 1 minute

1.   Variation:
T: Plays 1st ball into the BH corner
     Plays 2nd ball into the FH corner (FH-P on the run)

Notes:
Trainer serves up the 2nd ball before pupil has hit the 1st ball with his FH: The
player should play both balls as a passing shot into the court. After each series
of 6 balls, the player should reach a steady pulse within 3 minutes, before a
second series is attempted; maximum of 2 or 3 series (each of six balls) to be
played.

Mark Philipoussis (Australia)

Pete Sampras (USA)

G Group Training (G 1)

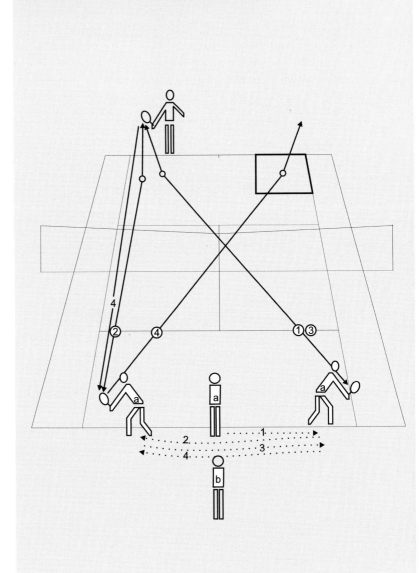

G 1 Groundstrokes

T: Feed from the baseline (FH side)
    1   = FH-CR
    2   = FH-LL
    3   = FH-CR
    4   = FH-LL

a: 1   = FH-CR
    2   = BH-LL
    3   = FH-CR
    4   = BH-CR-Winner (into target area)
b: Same as a

Aim: Groundst rokes (percentage, power-play, length, change of pace)

Intensity: High

Time: Approx 5-8 minutes

1. **Variation:**
T: Feed from the baseline (FH side)
    1   = FH-LL
    2   = FH-CR
    3   = FH-LL
    4   = FH-CR

a: 1   = BH-LL
    2   = FH-CR
    3   = BH-LL
    4   = FH-LL-Winner (into target area)

2. **Variation:**
T: Feed 1-4 from the net (either FH or BH side)
a: 1-4 as above

Notes:
Concentration on percentage and precision of the groundstrokes, change of pace (differing speed between groundstroke and winner). Accurate and fast feeds must be served up by the trainer. Different BH strokes possible (slice or top spin).

G

Group Training (G 2)

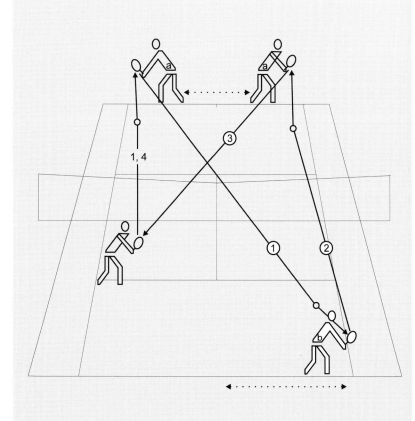

G 2 Groundstrokes

T: Feed from the net (BH side)
    1   = Feed LL to a
    4   = V-LL to a
    etc.

a: 1,4 = FH-CR to b
    3,5 = BH-CR to T
    etc.
b: 2,5 = FH-LL to a
    etc.

Aim: Groundstrokes (percentage, rhythm, precision)

Intensity: a: High
            b: Medium

Time: Approx 5-8 minutes

1.   Variation:
T: Feed from the net (FH side)
    1   = Feed LL to a
    3   = V-CR to a
    etc.

a: 1   = BH-LL to T
    3   = FH-LL to b
    etc.
b: 2   = BH-CR to a
    4   = BH-CR to a
    etc.

Notes:
Groundstroke percentage, precision and rhythm for both players; Player b must touch a point on the baseline after each stroke, which must be made on the move; Player b concentrates on the stroke; Player a exercises both types of strokes. Trainer functions both as server and feed server (determines the rate of play).

G Group Training (G 3)

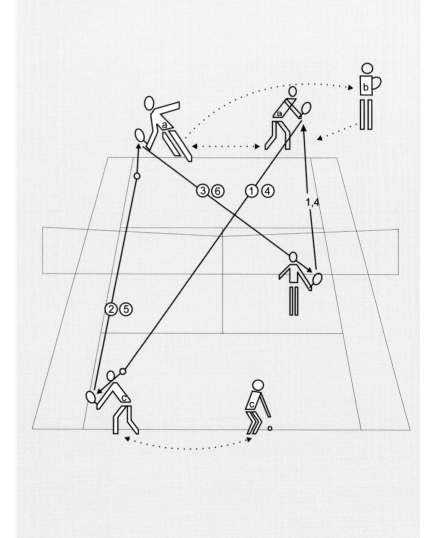

G 3 Groundstrokes

T: Feed from the net (FH side)
    1   = Feed LL
    4   = V-LL
    etc.

a(b): 1,4 = BH-CR to c
     3,6 = FH-CR to T
     etc.   (Change after 4 or 6 strokes)
c: 2 + 5 = BH-LL to a(b)
        (touch point on the baseline after each stroke)

Aim: Groundstrokes (percentage, rhythm, precision)

Intensity: High

Time: Approx 5 minutes

1. Variation:
T: Feed from the net (FH side)
    1   = Feed CR
    4   = V-CR
    etc.

b(a): 2   = BH-LL to c
     5   = FH-LL to T
     etc.   (Change after 4 strokes)
c: 3 + 6 = FH-CR to a(b)
     etc.   (touch point on the baseline after each stroke)

Notes:
Similar exercise to G 2. Percentage and precision of groundstrokes on the move, intense exercise for a and b; Player c exercises a groundstroke (strength and weakness ?), trainer determines rate of play!

G Group Training (G 4)

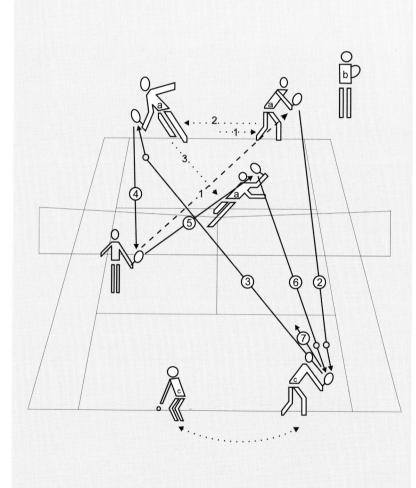

G 4 Groundstrokes / Attacking Ball / Volley

T: Feed from the net (BH side)
    1   = Feed CR
    5   = V-CR onto a's BH

c: 3   = FH-CR
    7   = P
        and play out the point (using the whole court)
a(b): 2   = BH-LL
    4   = FH-LL
    6   = BH-A-LL
        and play out the point (at the net position)

Aim: Groundstrokes
         Attacking ball
         Volley
         Passing shot (match play)

Intensity: a(b): High
          c: Medium-high

Time: Approx 5-10 minutes

Variation:
T: Feed from the net (FH side)
    1   = into FH corner (net)

c: 3   = BH-CR
    7   = BH-P
        and play out the point (using the whole court)
a(b): 2   = FH-LL
    4   = BH-LL
    6   = FH-A-LL
        and play out the point (at the net position)

Notes:
A demanding exercise with high intensity rate. Passing shot or lob also playable
by Player c. Trainer must determine speed and rhythm; Player a and b polish up
the backhand attacking ball, intensive foot work, concentration level is high.

G   Group Training (G 5)

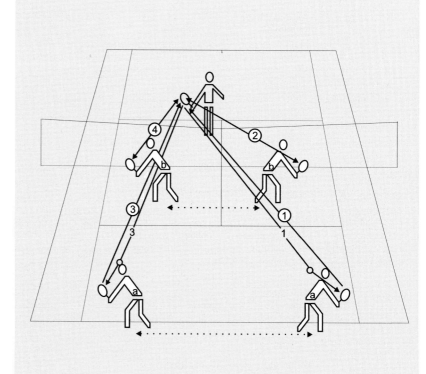

G 5 Groundstrokes / Volley

T: Feed from the net (T-line) onto the FH side
    1   = Feed (V-)CR to a
    2   = V-CR to b
    3   = V-LL to a
    4   = V-LL to b   etc.

a: 1   = FH-CR to T
    3   = BH-LL to T etc.
b: 2   = FH-V to T
    4   = BH-V to T   etc.

Aim: Groundstrokes (percentage, rhythm)
            Volley (power-play, percentage, leg work, mobility)

Intensity: a: High
            b: Medium-high

Time: Approx 5 minutes

1.   Variation:
T: Feed from the net (T-line) onto the BH side
    1   = Feed (V-)CR to a
    2   = V-LL to a
    3   = V to b
    4   = V to b   etc.

a: 1   = BH-CR to T
    3   = FH-LL to T etc.
b: 2   = BH-V to T
    4   = FH-V to T   etc.

2.   Variation:
Player a or b replaces T's position
(T takes up b's volley position)

Notes:
Exercise suited to begin a training session. Demanding task for the trainer (volley technique!); Player b plays on the volley side where otherwise the groundstroke would have been played; Player a plays accurate groundstrokes (90% speed); Player b plays forcing volleys (leg work).

G Group Training (G 6)

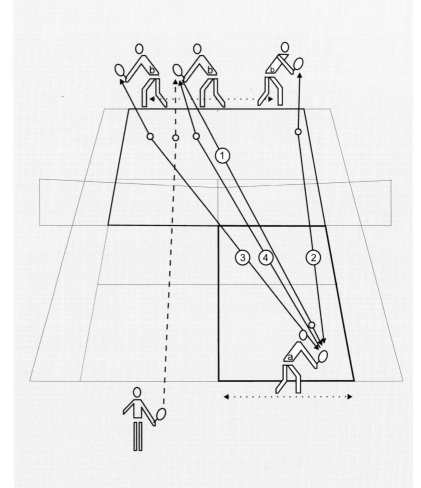

G 6 Groundstrokes

T: Feed to b

a: 1+... = FH at will – into the whole of b's marked target area
b: 1-4 = FH or BH only into a's FH corner (marked target area)

Aim: Groundstrokes (percentage, accuracy, power-play)

Intensity: a: Low
            b: High

Time: Approx 5 minutes

Variation:
Play for points (11 points)
Player b can play attacking shots
(Once the attacking shot has been played the whole of a's court is open)

Notes:
Exercise, with high demands, simulating match play, in particular for Player b, who has to cover the whole of the Singles court area while Player a concentrates on the groundstroke. When using the variation form, Player b can respond to a short ball from player a by attacking into either corner. In this case, Player a exercises the passing shot.

G Group Training (G 7)

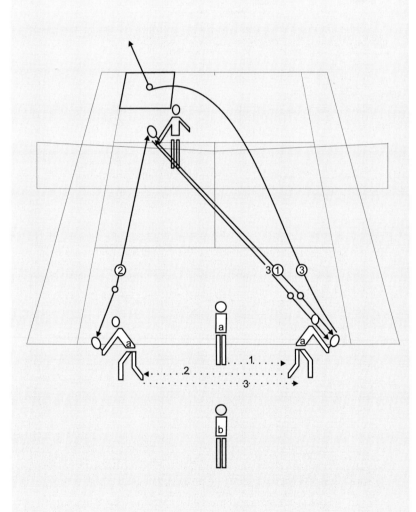

G 7 Groundstrokes / Special Strokes

T: Feeds 1-3 from the net (FH side)

a: 1   = FH-CR to T
       2   = BH-LL to T
       3   = FH-TSP-LOB-CR (into target area)

b: Same as a

Aim: Groundstrokes
             Special strokes (technique)

Intensity: High

Time: Approx 8-10 minutes

Variation:
T: Feeds 1-4 from the net (FH side)

a,b: 1   = BH-LL
      2   = FH-CR
      3   = BH-LOB-LL (into marked target area)
      4   = FH-LL-Winner

Notes:
Groundstroke rhythm, concentration on special strokes (top spin-lob). Trainer must exercise optimum timing for the feed (top spin-lob and winner should be played on the move!). With 2 or 3 players make a changeover whenever a mistake is made in groundstrokes 1 and 2 (concentration on percentage is thus underlined).

G   Group Training (G 8)

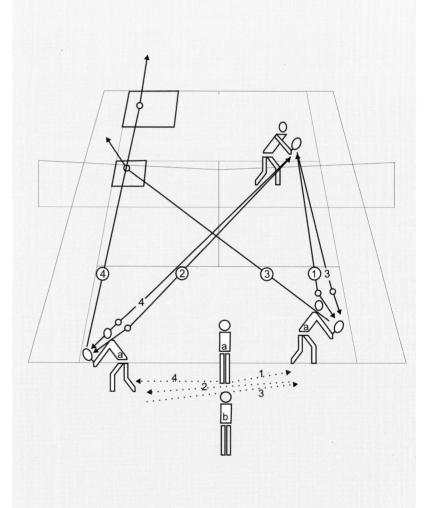

G 8 Groundstrokes / Special Strokes

T: Feeds 1-4 from the net (BH side)
      1   = into a's (b's) FH corner
      2   = into a's (b's) BH corner
      3   = into a's (b's) FH corner
           (angle for short-CR!)
      4   = into a's (b's) BH corner (fast feed)

a: 1   = FH-LL to T
      2   = BH-CR to T
      3   = FH-Short-CR (into target area)
      4   = BH-Winner (into target area)
b: Same as a

Aim: Groundstrokes
            Special strokes

Intensity: High

Time: Approx 10 minutes

Variation:
T: Feeds 1-4 from the net (FH side)

a,b: 1   = BH-LL to T
      2   = FH-CR to T
      3   = BH-TSP-Short-CR
      4   = FH-TSP-LOB-CR

Notes:
Safe groundstrokes; polishing special strokes (change of speed for the short cross and winner strokes!. Timing of the trainer's feeds is important (T must feed accurately and return the volley with precision). Mark the target areas with ball canisters.

G Group Training (G 9)

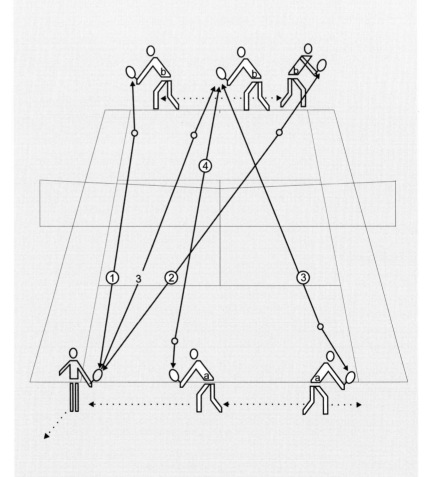

G 9 Groundstrokes

T: 1   = Feed from the baseline (BH side)
    2   = Feed into b's BH corner
    3   = Feed into b's FH corner
         (T leaves the court area)

b: 1   = FH-LL to T
    2   = BH-CR to T
    3   = FH or BH to a
    4   = Play out the point using the singles court area (up to 11 points)
a: 3 + 4 = Play out the point

Aim: Groundstrokes (percentage, power-play) played in a match style

Intensity: b: High
         a: Medium-high

Time: Approx 8-10 minutes

Variation:
T: Feed from the baseline (FH side)

b: 1   = BH-LL to T
    2   = FH-CR to T
    3   = Play out the point with a (up to 11 points)
a: 3 + 4 = Play out the point

Notes:
Suitable exercise for the beginning of training (possible to include 3 players).
Emphasis on stroke and running rhythm; match simulating exercise.

G Group Training (G 10)

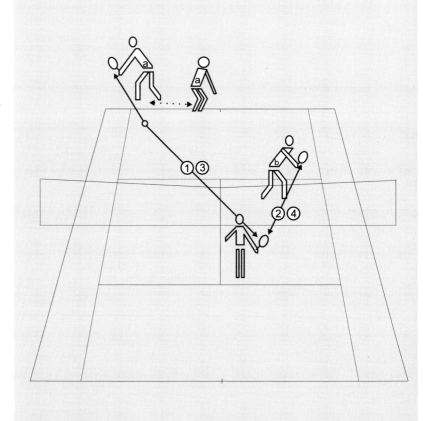

G 10   Groundstrokes / Volley

T: Feed from the net
1 + 3 = Feed into a's FH corner
2 + 4 = Feed to b (net position)
etc.

a: 1 + 3 = FH to T
(after each FH play, touch the baseline mid-point)
etc.
b: 2 + 4 = V to T
etc.

Aim: Groundstrokes (percentage, power-play, leg work)
Volleys (reaction, leg work, mobility)

Intensity: a: High
b: Medium

Time: Approx 5-8 minutes

Variation:
T: Feed from the BH side (net)

a: 1 + 3 = BH-CR to T
etc.
b: 2 + 4 = V to T
etc.

Notes:
Player a concentrates on the groundstroke (strength/weakness), but must hit the ball on the move (the distance to be crossed can be lengthened); Player b moves on each volley shot (playing FH or BH volley). Trainer must be able to determine rate of volley returns; a 3rd player can take the place of the trainer.

G Group Training (G 11)

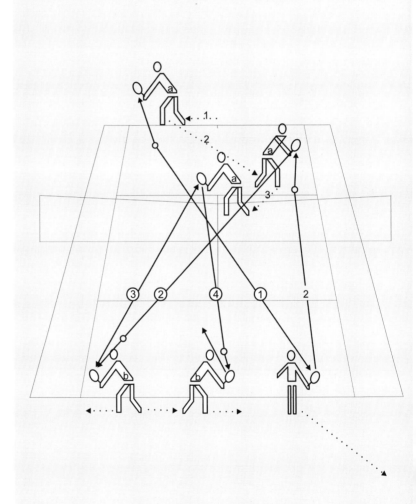

G 11   Attacking Ball / Volley / Passing Shot

T: Feed from the baseline (FH side)
  1   = Feed into a's FH corner
  2   = Feed onto the T-line (a's BH corner)

a: 1   = FH-CR to T
  2   = BH-A to b
  3   = V (LL or CR)
  4   = Play out the point at the net
b: 3   = FH or BH to a
  4   = Play out the point (from the baseline/ with P)

Aim: Attacking ball
        Volley
        Passing shot (played in a match style)

Intensity: a: High
        b: Medium

Time: Approx 5 minutes

Variation:
T: Feed from the baseline (BH side)

a: 1   = BH-CR to T
  2   = FH-A-CR to b
  3   = V (LL or CR)
  4   = Play out the point (at the net)
b: 3   = FH or BH to a
  4   = Play out the point (from the baseline/with P)

Notes:
Combined exercise with Player a using a complex assortment of strokes; Player b must free himself from the defensive position (passing shots!).

G Group Training (G 12)

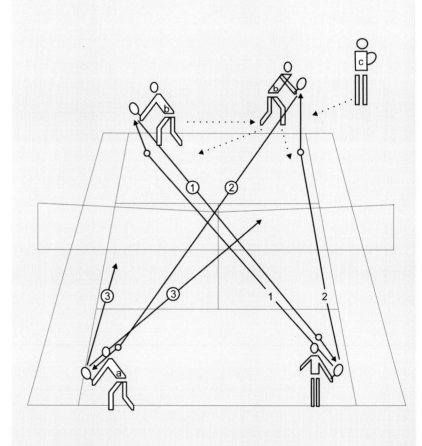

G 12   Groundstrokes

T: Feed from the baseline (FH side)
       1   = Feed into b's FH corner
       2   = Feed into b's BH corner
b: 1   = FH-CR to T
       2   = BH-CR to a
       3   = Play out the point (from the baseline)
              (to 11 points/with a together)
c: Same as b
a: 3   = BH-CR or BH-LL and play out the point

Aim: Groundstrokes (variation of slice and top spin)
Intensity: With 2 players – high
                With 3 players – medium
Time: Approx 5-8 minutes

1.   Variation:
T: Feed from the baseline (BH side)
       1   = Feed into b's BH corner
       2   = Feed into b's FH corner
b: 1   = FH/CC/BH (from the BH corner)
       2   = FH-CR to c
       3   = Play out the point (to 11 points/with a together)
c: Same as b
a: 3   = FH-CR or FH-LL and play out the point

2.   Variation:
T: Feed from the baseline (FH side)
       1   = Feed into b's FH corner
       2   = Feed into b's BH corner
b: 1   = FH-LL to T
       2   = BH-LL to c
       3   = Play out the point
c: Same as b
a: 3   = FH-LL or FH-CR and play out the point

Notes:
Percentage, power-play and variation of the groundstrokes (Slice/Top spin) in competition simulating conditions. Trainer dictates the rhythm with his 2 feeds. Each mistake counts (loss of points). Accurate feed by the trainer is required.

G Group Training (G 13)

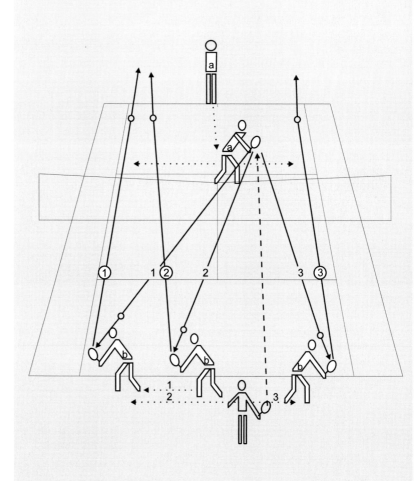

G 13   Groundstrokes

T: Feed onto a's BH (T-line)

a: BH-SL (at will)
   1   = BH-SL-A-CR
   2   = BH-SL-A into the middle (aim at b's body)
   3   = BH-SL-A-LL
b: 1 - 3 = P-LL or P-CR

Aim: Attacking ball
   Passing shot (match style)

Intensity: High

Time: Approx 10 minutes

1.   Variation:
a: 4th possibility = BH-A-STOP
b: P or LOB

2.   Variation:
a: FH-A into b's BH corner or FH corner

Notes:
Exercise with match style characteristics (each player hits 20-30 passing shots).
After each point the passing shot player must return to the start position
(centre of the baseline). Trainer's feed is played at speed onto the T-line area of
the attacking player.

G Group Training (G 14)

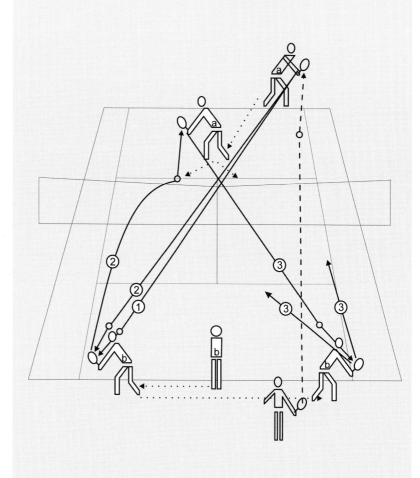

G 14   Backhand Variations / Attacking Ball / Passing Shots

T: 1   = Feed into a's BH corner
a: 1 + 2 = BH-CR (TSP or SL)
   3   = FH-A-CR
   4   = V-CR or V-LL and play out the point

b: 1   = BH-CR (TSP or SL)
   2   = BH as a feed into the T-line area
   3   = FH-P-CR or FH-P-LL and play out the point

Aim: Backhand Variations (percentage, length)
        Attacking ball
        Volley
        Passing shot (played in a match style)

Intensity: High

Time: Approx 5-8 minutes

1.   Variation:
a: 1 + 2 = FH/CC/BH (from the BH corner)
   3   = BH-A-LL
   4   = V and play out the point
b: 1   = BH-CR
   2   = BH-CR (onto a's T-line)
   3   = FH-P-CR or FH-P-LL
   T   = feed into a's BH corner

2.   Variation:
a: 1 + 2 = FH-TSP-CR
   3   = BH-A-CR
   4   = V and play out the point
b: 1   = FH-TSP-CR
   2   = FH-LL (onto a's T-line)
   3   = BH-P-CR or BH-P-LL or LOB and play out the point

Notes:
Exercise points are: percentage, power play and groundstroke accuracy; groundstroke variations: Player a offensive, while Player b must free himself from a defensive position. Disadvantage: Player b is required to play the 2nd ball as a feed ball (T-line).

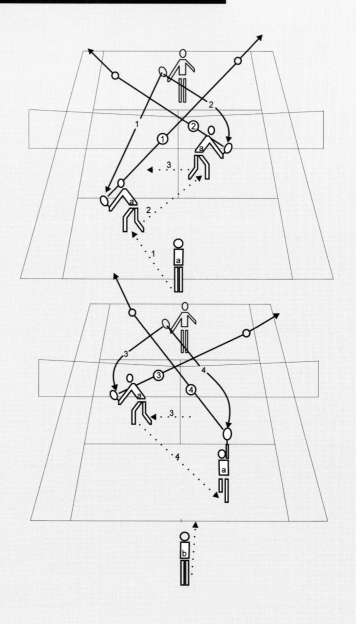

G Group Training (G 15)

G 15   Attacking Ball / Volley / Smash

T: Feed 1 (from T-line/middle onto a's BH)
      2   = Low feed onto FH
      3   = Low feed onto BH
      4   = LOB

a+b: 1   = BH-A-SL
      2   = FH-V-CR (low)
      3   = FH-V-CR (low)
      4   = S (while running backwards) into the FH corner

Aim: Attacking ball
            Volley
            Smash (leg work, mobility)

Intensity: High

Time: With 2 players – approx 6 minutes
          With 3 players – approx 10 minutes

1. Variation:
a+b: 1   = FH-A-TSP-CR
      2   = BH-V-LL
      3   = S (outwards)
      4   = FH-V-LL
      5   = S (outwards)

T: Feed from the T-line (middle)

2. Variation:
a+b: 1   = BH-A-SL-CR
      2   = FH-V-STOP
      3   = BH-V-STOP
      4   = S (while running backwards)

T: Feed from the baseline (BH side)

Notes:
Drill exercise suitable for up to 4 players (rotation method). The trainer must provide fast and accurate feed balls (timing). Emphasis on net play training (mobility).

G Group Training (G 16)

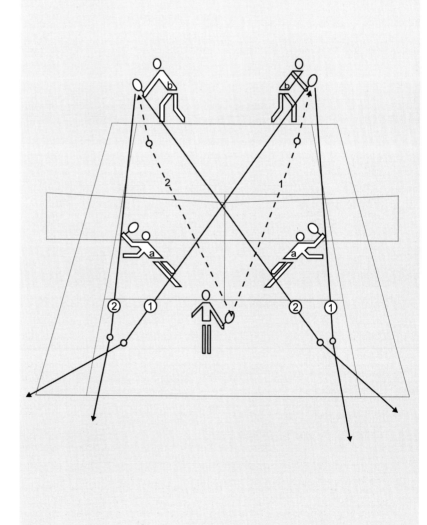

G 16   Passing Shots / Volley

T: Feed, alternately, into b's FH or BH corner

b: 1   = BH-P-CR or BH-P-LL
              (alternately, no lobs)
      2   = FH-P-CR or FH-P-LL
              (alternately, no lobs)
a: 1+2+... = V into the singles court area

Aim: Passing shot, played on the run
              Volley (reaction), played in a match style

Intensity: b: High
              a: Medium-high

Time: Approx 3 minutes

Variation:
b: 1   = BH-P-CR or BH-P-LL or BH-LOB
      2   = FH-P-CR or FH-P-LL or FH-LOB
a: 1+2+... = V onto a target (ball canister in the service area) or S

Notes:
Match simulating exercise; Player b has to achieve 10 clear passing shots without player a having touched the ball. Trainer should exercise flexibility in the number of passing shots to be played because of the high rate of intensity required (anaerobic phase/rest pauses must be maintained). Trainer must serve up fast and accurate feed balls.

Michael Stich (Germany)

Malivai Washington (USA)

G Group Training (G 17)

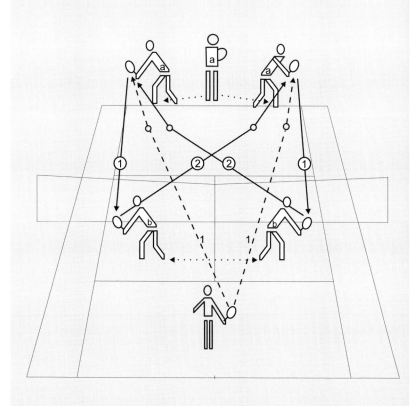

G 17   Passing Shots / Volley

T: Feed, alternately, into a's FH or BH corner

a: 1 = BH-P-LL or FH-P-LL
    2 = FH-P (at will), or, BH-P (at will)
       and play out the point

b: 2 = FH-V-CR or BH-V-CR
       and play out the point

Aim: Passing shot, played on the run
           Volley (mobility at the net)

Intensity: High

Time: Approx 3-5 minutes

Variation:
a: 1 = FH-P-LL or BH-P-LL
    2 = Play out the point
b: 1 = FH-V-CR or FH-V-LL
       (BH-V-CR or BH-V-LL)
       and play out the point

Notes:
Trainer must serve up fast and accurate feed balls. Player a must be prepared in the opposite corner immediately after playing the 1st ball; Player b volleys cross court as hard as possible, even if Player b doesn't reach the ball (match simulation). Maintain the recovery rest breaks!

G | Group Training (G 18)

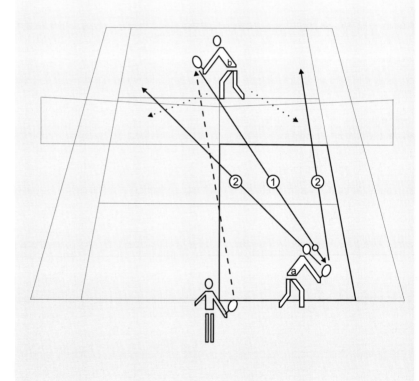

G 18   Volley / Passing Shot

T: Feed to b

b: 1   = FH-V or BH-V into the marked target area
           and play out the point
           (whole of the singles court)

a: 2   = FH-P-CR or FH-P-LL
           and play out the point from the FH corner
           (half of the singles court)

Aim: Volley
           Passing – played in a match style

Intensity: High

Time: Approx 5 minutes

Variation:
b: 1   = FH-V or BH-V into a's BH corner
           and play out the point
           (whole of the singles court)

a: 2   = BH-P-CR or BH-P-LL
           and play out the point from the BH corner
           (half of the singles court)

Notes:
Match simulation (for points) exercising volleys and passing shots against the clock. Watch for b's starting position before each point – T-line!. Trainer requires to provide accurate and quick feed balls.

G Group Training (G 19)

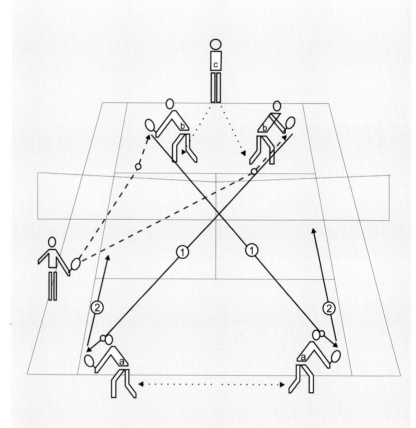

G 19   Attacking Ball / Passing Shot

T: Feed into the T-line area

b,c: 1   = FH-A-CR or BH-A-CR
      2   = V
            and play out the point
a: 2   = FH-P (at will)
            or BH-P (at will)
            and play out the point

Aim: Attacking ball
            Passing shot played on the run

Intensity: a: High
            b: Medium-high

Time: Approx 8-10 minutes

1.   Variation:
T: Feed into the T-line area

b,c: 1   = FH-A-LL or BH-A-LL
      2   = V
            and play out the point
a: 2   = FH-P or BH-P
            and play out the point

2.   Variation:
T: High feed onto b' or c's FH (T-line)

b,c: 1   = FH-A onto a's body
            and play out the point
a: 2   = FH-P or BH-P

Notes:
Ideal exercise for match simulation for 2-4 players. Concentration on a variety of attacking shots with the transition to the volley; player making the passing shot must free himself from a defensive position. Player a may only leave his start position (middle) when the ball has been played. Each player carries out 30 passing shots (rotation method).

G Group Training (G 20)

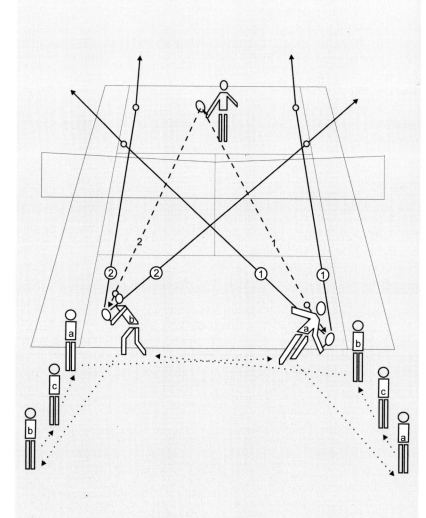

G 20   Passing Shot

T: Feed alternately into the FH and BH corner

a,b,c: 1   = FH-P-LL or FH-P-CR
                   (at will, into the singles court area)
             2   = BH-P-LL or BH-P-CR
                   (at will, into the singles court area)

Aim: Passing shot played on the run

Intensity: High

Time: Approx 5-8 minutes

1.   Variation:
T: Calls out the stroke direction to be played as he feeds

a,b,c: Attempt to hit a ball canister in the FH and BH corner

2.   Variation:
T: Calls out further stroke variations

a,b,c: FH-P-Short-CR, BH-P-Short-CR
             or FH-TSP-LOB, BH-TSP-LOB

Notes:
Trainer must provide fast and accurate feed balls (timing). Player's concentration
is challenged, as direction of ball play is first called out by the trainer on the feed.
Players must move in the area near to the baseline (small steps).

G Group Training (G 21)

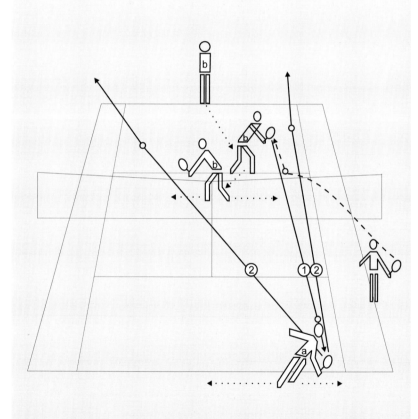

G 21   Attacking Ball / Passing Shot

T: Feed from the T-line (from outside the court)

b: 1   = BH-A-LL and play out the point (from the net)
a: 2   = FH-P-LL or FH-P-CR (at will)
           and play out the point (from the baseline/whole court)

Aim: Attacking ball (percentage, accuracy, power-play)
           Passing shot (speed)

Intensity: Medium-high

Time: Approx 10 minutes each player (per passing shot side)

1.   Variation:
b: 1   = BH-SL-A-CR and play out the point
a: 2   = BH-P-LL or BH-P-CR and play out the point

2.   Variation:
b: 1   = FH-A-CR and play out the point
a: 2   = FH-P-LL or FH-P-CR and play out the point

3.   Variation:
b: 1   = FH-A-LL and play out the point
a: 2   = BH-P-LL or BH-P-CR and play out the point

4.   Variation:
T: Medium height feed to b (b plays approaching shot with a V)
b: 1   = V-A at a's body (middle court/baseline)
a: 2   = FH-P or BH-P (at will)

5.   Variation:
T: High feed onto the T-line
       (Ball bounces up (unlike 4th variation)
b: 1   = FH-A at a's body (middle court/baseline)
a: 2   = FH-P or BH-P (at will)

Notes:
Match simulating exercise (each player makes 20-30 passing shots/rotation
method). For all variations (except the 4th and 5th) the trainer must provide a
quick low feed ball just behind the T-line; Player a may only start when the
attacking ball has been played – as in a match.

G Group Training (G 22)

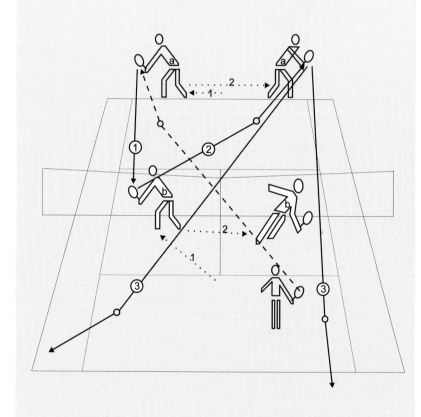

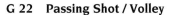

G 22   Passing Shot / Volley

T: Feed into a's FH corner

a: 1   = FH-LL to b
      3   = BH-P-LL (at will)
             or BH-P-CR (at will)
             and play out the point (from the baseline)
b: 2   = V into a's BH corner
             and play out the point (net position)

Aim: Passing shot – played in a match style
             Volley

Intensity: a: High
             b: Medium-high

Time: Approx 5 minutes each player (per passing shot side)

Variation:
T: Feed into a's BH corner

a: 1   = BH-LL to b
      3   = FH-P-LL or FH-P-CR
             and play out the point (baseline)
b: 2   = V into a's FH corner
             and play out the point (net position)

Notes:
Passing shot exercise under match conditions; Player a must free himself from the defensive position with a passing shot; Player b exercises the Volley (balance, mobility, position control on the volley).

G ₀ Group Training (G 23)

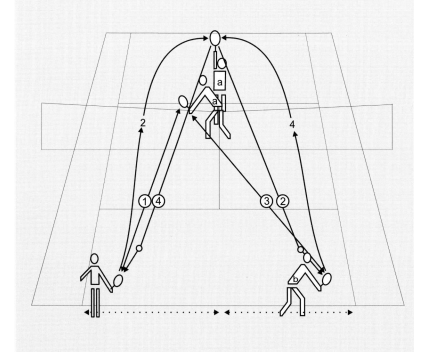

G 23   Volley / Smash

T: 1   = Low feed (Player a volleys)
     2   = High feed (Player a smashes)

b: 3   = Low feed (Player a volleys)
     4   = High feed (Player a smashes)
a: 1   = V to T
     2   = S to b
     3   = V to b
     4   = S to T
     etc.

Aim: Volley (leg work, mobility, balance)
                Smash (mobility, power-play)

Intensity: a: High
               b: Low

Time: Approx 5 minutes

Notes:
Suitable exercise also for 3 players (c takes place of T); player a must cover the whole net area. Trainer counts the perfect ball exchanges of each player (change-overs as per rotation method). Player a: high intensity training (maintain recovery rest pauses).

G Group Training (G 24)

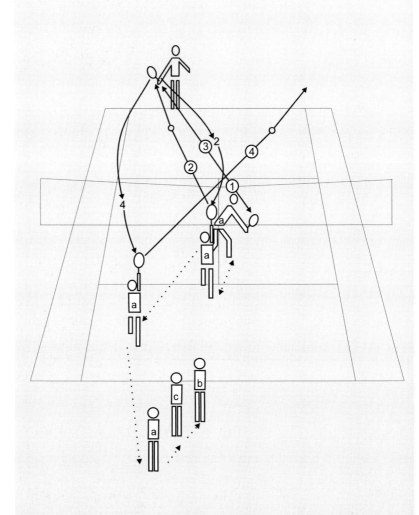

G 24   Volley / Smash

T: Feed from the FH corner
    1   = Low feed
    2   = High feed
    3   = Low feed
    4   = High feed

a: 1   = V to T
    2   = S to T
    3   = V to T
    4   = S into open corner

b,c: as for a

Aim: Volley (mobility, balance, power-play)
            Smash (leg work, mobility)

Intensity: High

Time: Approx 8-10 minutes

Variation:
T: Feed from BH corner
    (Low or high alternately)

a: 1   = V to T (BH corner)
    2   = S to T
    3   = V-STOP
    4   = S into open corner (running backwards)

Notes:
Exercise can be varied at will (e.g. backhand-smash, top spin volley or make player chase the lob). Trainer's capability to serve good feeds is important (percentage, precision and timing). Also suitable for singles training – (see S 14).

G | Group Training (G 25)

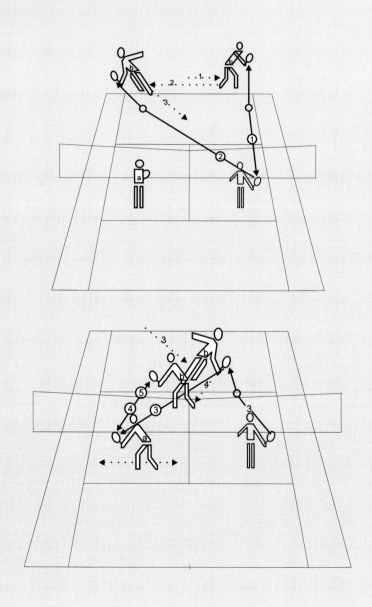

G 25   Groundstrokes

T: Feed from the net/FH corner

b: 1   = BH-LL to T
      2   = FH-CR to T
      3   = BH-SL-A to a
      4,5... = V duel with a
a: 4,5... = V duel with b

Aim: Groundstrokes (power-play)
           Attacking ball (percentage, speed)
           Volley (leg work, reaction)

Intensity: b: High
             a: Low

Time: Approx 5-10 minutes

Variation:
T: Feed from the net/BH corner

b: 1   = BH-CR to T
      2   = FH-LL to T
      3   = BH-SL-A to a
      4,5...= V duel with a for points
a: 4,5...= V duel with b for points

Notes:
Complex exercise with a high technical level. Trainer must deliver accurate and precise feed balls. Match simulation using point scoring; rotation method for three players.

115

G Group Training (G 26)

G 26   Volley

T: Feed alternately to a and b (from the net position)

a: 1   = FH-V to T
      3   = BH-V to T
b: 2   = V (at will) to T
               (b: 1-2 m from the net)
      4   = V (at will) to T

Aim: Volley (percentage, leg work, reaction)

Intensity: a: High
                    b: Low

Time: Approx 5 minutes per player

Variation:
T: Volley feed 1+3 low (just behind the net)

a: 1   = FH-V (low) to T
      3   = BH-V (low) to T
b: 2   = V (at will) to T
      4   = V (at will) to T

Notes:
Basic exercise for the improvement of the volley; reaction and leg work for the
high and low volley. Trainer determines the speed and height of the volley.
Trainer can adjust his net position (FH or BH side).

G Group Training (G 27)

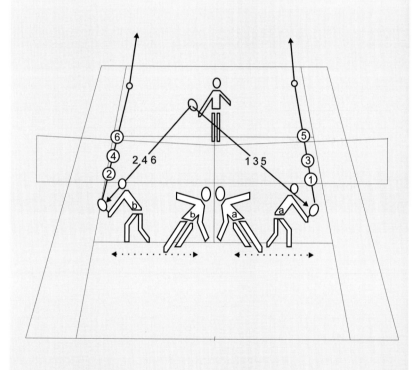

G 27   Volley

T: Feed alternately to a and b (from the net position)

a: 1,3,5 = FH-V-LL
b: 2,4,6 = BH-V-LL
            (a and b touch the middle line after each volley)

Aim: Volley (leg work, speed)

Intensity: High

Time: Approx 3-5 minutes per side

1.   Variation:
a: 1,3,5... = FH-V-CR
b: 2,4,6... = BH-V-CR

2.   Variation:
a: 1,3,5... = BH-V (low)
b: 2,4,6... = FH-V (low)

3.   Variation:
a: 1,3,5... = FH-V (high)
b: 2,4,6... = BH-V (high)

Notes:
Large variety of volley training (drop volley also possible). Trainer determines speed and height of the feed; Players (a,b) change sides after each series; recovery rest pauses!

G Group Training (G 28)

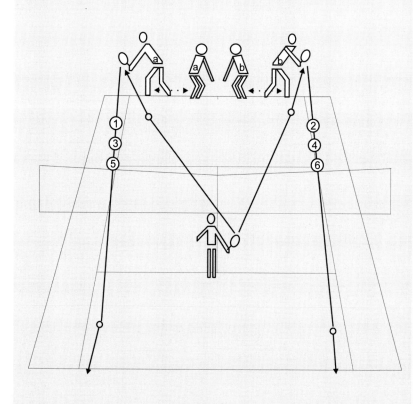

G 28   Passing Shot

T: Feed alternately to a and b (from the T-line position)

a: 1,3,5 = FH-P-LL
        (and touch the middle line)
b: 2,4,6 = BH-P-LL
        (and touch the middle line)

Aim: Passing shot (relief of the defence)

Intensity: High

Time: Approx 3-5 minutes per side

Variation:
P-Short-CR or TSP-LOB

Notes:
Intensive drill exercise of a stroke (passing shot) against the clock. Demands leg work, speed and coordination. A recovery rest break is recommended after 15-20 strokes. Trainer determines the rate of play.

G Group Training (G 29)

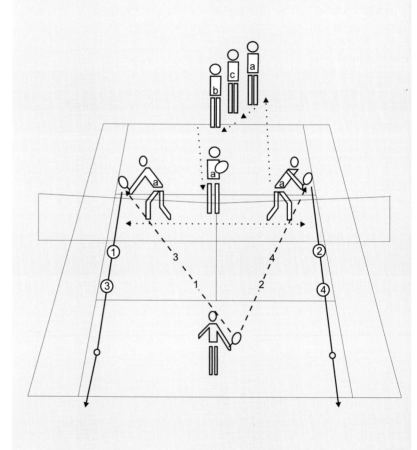

G 29   Volley

T: Feed alternately onto FH and BH

a: 1   = FH-V-LL
      2   = BH-V-LL
      3   = FH-V-LL
      4   = BH-V-LL (Afterwards the player picks up the 4 balls)
b,c: same as a

Aim: Volley (leg work, speed)

Intensity: High

Time: Approx 10 minutes

1.   Variation:

a,b,c: 1   = FH-V-CR
          2   = BH-V-CR
          3   = FH-V-STOP-CR
          4   = BH-V-STOP-CR
               (Afterwards the player picks up the balls)

2.   Variation:
a,b,c: 4 Volleys without T giving previous indication of direction

Notes:
Drill training exercise, 3 players optimum. Trainer must use quick feeds – similar to those in a match. Additional condition training aspect for the players (ball collection). Maintain recovery rest breaks!

G Group Training (G 30)

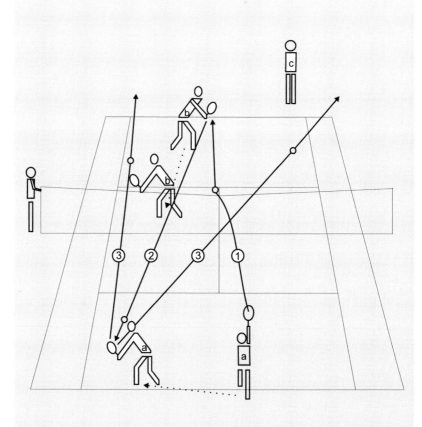

G 30   Service / Return / Volley

a: 1   = 2nd service onto b's BH (from deuce side)
    3   = BH-P-LL or BH-P-CR
        and play out the point
b: 2   = RETURN as a BH-A into a's BH corner and play out the point (from
        the net position) and afterwards, as above, from the advantage side
c: as for b

Aim: 2nd Service (twist or slice)
         Return
         Volley (as played in a match)

Intensity: High

Time: Approx 10 minutes (then change of server)

1.   Variation:
a: 1   = 2nd service alternately from the deuce and advantage side
    3   = FH-P or BH-P and play out the point
b: 2   = BH-RETURN as a BH-A into either of a's corners
        and play out the point (from the net position)

2.   Variation:
a: 1   = 2nd service onto b's FH
    3   = FH-P or BH-P and play out the point
b: 2   = FH-RETURN as a FH-A into either of a's corners
        and play out the point (from the net position)

Notes:
Exercise for the practice of the 2nd service (twist or slice) and relief out of the
defensive position using passing shots. Chip and charge exercises for the return
player, who is forced to make an offensive return (especially on fast surfaces).
Trainer gives tactical and technical tips to both players.

G Group Training (G 31)

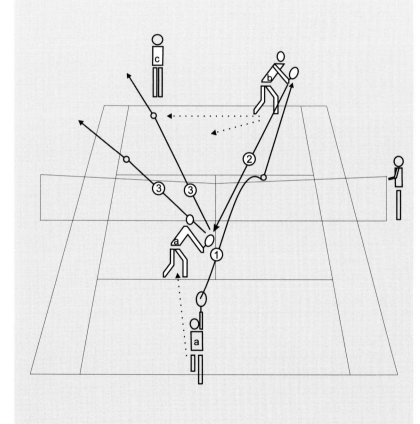

G 31   Service / Return / Volley

a: 1 = 1st and 2nd service (from the advantage side) onto b's body
    3 = V into b's FH corner
       and play out the point (net position)
b: 2 = RETURN (low/onto a's feet)
       and play out the point (from the baseline)
       Follow on:
a: 1 = 1st and 2nd service (from the deuce side) at will
    3 = V into b's BH corner
       and play out the point (net position)
b: 2 = RETURN anywhere in the court
       and play out the point (from the baseline)

Aim: Service
           Volley
           Return (as played in a match)

Intensity: High

Time: Approx 10 minutes

Variation:
a: 1 = 1st and 2nd service
    3 = V-Stop
       and play out the point
b: 2 = RETURN anywhere on the court
       and play out the point

Notes:
Exercise form for the improvement of the serve and volley under match conditions (normal scoring); Player b plays the return onto Player a's feet (return block). Player a must cover the whole court from the net position.

Albert Costa (Spain)

Todd Woodbridge (Australia)

D Doubles Training (D 1)

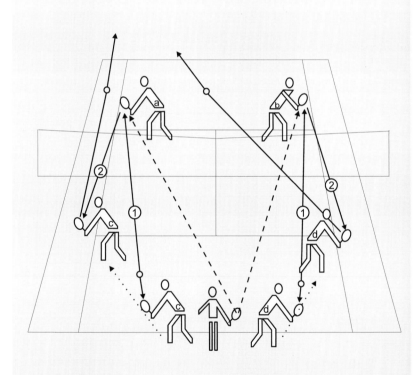

D 1 Doubles Tactics

T: Feed alternately to a and b (baseline/middle)

a+b: 1   = V to c or d (start position T-line)
       2   = V and play out the point (each team 30 points)
c+d: 1,2... = P (at will)
              and play out the point

Aim: Doubles tactics
            on the offensive (a+b) and
            in defence (c+d), as in a match

Intensity: Medium-high

Time: Approx 10-15 minutes per team

Notes:
Complex exercise in which all the technical and tactical elements of doubles
can be used. The doubles couple should develop a mutual strategy (covering
the whole court from the net position (for a+b) and at the baseline (for c+d)).
The team should position themselves level! Tactical variations for c+d: lob,
forehand and backhand through the centre, low groundstrokes, forehand into
the cross court (short) or backhand into the cross court (short). Tactical variations
for a+b: volley with length and accuracy, drop volley. Change roles after 30
points.

D Doubles Training (D 2)

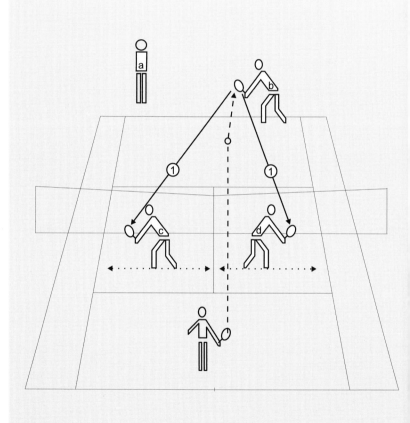

D 2 Forehand-Winner / Volley

T: Feed – medium height – alternately to a's and b's FH

a,b: 1   = FH-Winner to c or FH-Winner to d
      2,3... = Play out the point (each team 30 points)
c+d: 2,3... = Play out the point (from the net position)

Aim: Leg work on the volley (mobility)
             Forehand-winner
             Doubles tactics
             on the offensive (a+b) and
             in defence (c+d), as in a match

Intensity: High

Time: Approx 10 minutes per team

Notes:
Exercise form, specifically for doubles, with match characteristics (30 points per team). Tactical play adapted to the situation in the defence (c and d must free themselves from the defence) and on the offensive (with a and b in an advantaged position).

D Doubles training (D 3)

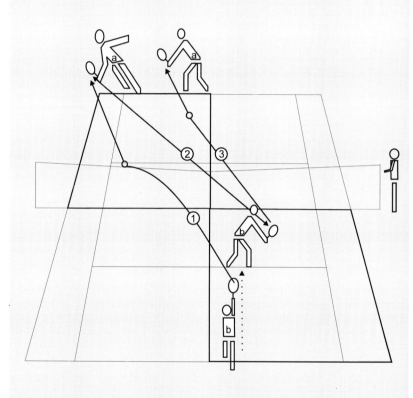

D 3 Service / Return / Volley

b: 1   = Service down the outside (onto a's FH)
    3   = V into marked target area
         and play out the point
a: 2   = RETURN-CR
    4   = Play out the point from the baseline (in the marked area)
         Follow on – service and RETURN onto the advantage side
         (Up to 11 points) – as in a match
c,d: Same as a and b

Aim: Service
             Volley
             Return onto same side (without doubles partner; strengths and
             weaknesses)

Intensity: Medium-high

Time: Approx 10-15 minutes

Variation:
a: Must follow up to the net after the RETURN (chip and charge), or the
     next stroke

Notes:
Exercise under match conditions (without partner). Practice of the most
important of the doubles strokes (service, return, volley). Covering from the one
court side (doubles court area). Points as per normal scoring also possible.

D Doubles Training (D 4)

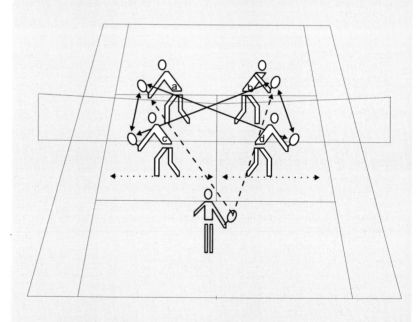

D 4 Volley

T: Feed to a and b

a+b: V to c and d (for points)
c,d: V to a and b (for points)

Aim: Volley (reaction, leg work)

Intensity: Low

Time: Approx 10 minutes

1.   Variation:
a+b: V-LL
c+d: V-CR

2.   Variation:
As 1st variation, but using 2 balls
(a and b play balls simultaneously)

Notes:
Typical exercise for net play practice (ball is played close to the body). Mutual coordination with partner in the net position. Aggressive volleying; reaction training. Trainer feeds and calls corrections.

D   Doubles Training (D 5)

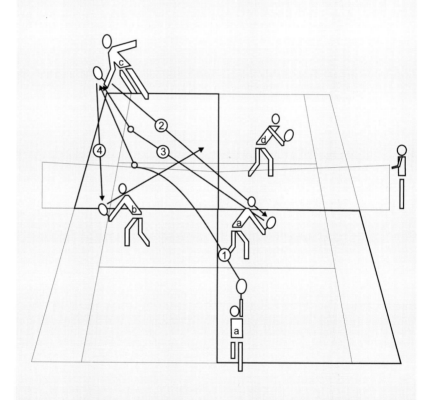

D 5 Service / Return / Volley

T: Gives comments from the sideline at the net
     (Technical and tactical tips)

a: 1   = 1st (2nd) Service onto c's FH (down the outside line)
     3   = V-CR
b: 2   = RETURN-CR
     4   = Play out the point (with a and d)
         Follow on – 1st (2nd) service onto d's BH
         and then the same stroke exchanges as above

Aim: Service
           Return
           Volley (mutual coordination with partner)

Intensity: Medium-high

Time: Approx 10 minutes for each serve player

Variation:
a: 1   = 1st (2nd) service onto c's BH
     3   = V-LL to d
     4   = Play out the point
c: 2   = RETURN-CR
         and play out the point

Notes:
Exercise in which the first 3 strokes are prescribed; 1st service can be played as if it were the 2nd service (twist/slice). Close up to the net quickly after the service. All strokes played under match conditions (speed of play).

D | Doubles Training (D 6)

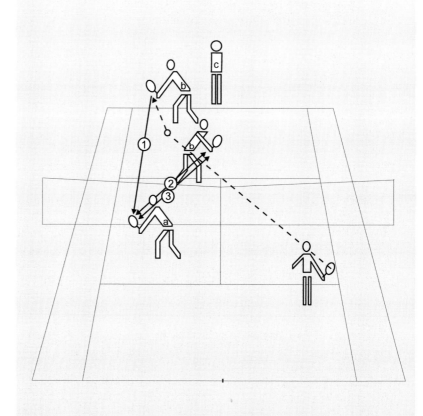

D 6   Volley

T: Feed – medium height – onto b's, c's FH etc

b: 1   = FH-Winner to a
        2,3... = V duel with a (in the one half of the court)
c: same as b
a: 2,3... = V duel with b (in the one half of the court)

Aim: Volley (power play, reaction)

Intensity: Medium-high

Time: Approx 10 minutes

1.   Variation:
b,c   FH-Winner and V into a's FH corner
        and V duel with a
a: V duel (from the FH corner)

2.   Variation:
b,c: BH-SL-A-LL to a
        and V duel with a
a: V duel (from the FH corner)

Notes:
Individual doubles exercise with varied distribution of tasks; Player b(c) must close up to the net rapidly; Player a, positioned at the net (approx 1-2 m in front of the T-line), must free himself from the defensive posture and close up to the net.

D Doubles Training (D 7)

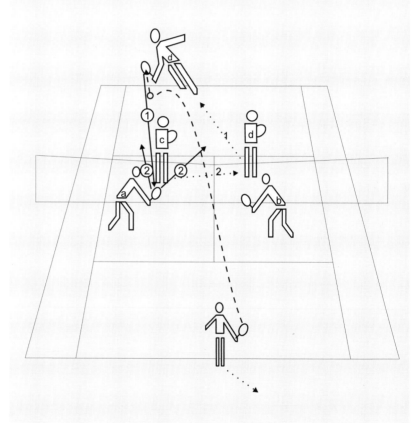

D 7   Doubles Tactics

T: Feed - Lob over c's head

d: 1   = Chase the lob (running diagonally backwards) and play FH to a
                (c changes over to d's side)
                and play out the point
a: 2 etc., = V
                and play out the point

Aim: Doubles tactics
                Switch from the offensive to the defensive (c and d)
                Coordination with partner
                Volley (power-play, reaction)

Intensity: a+b: Medium
                c+d: Medium-high

Time: Approx 5-10 minutes per team

Variation:
c: 1   = Gather the lob (d runs back to the baseline)
a+b: 2   = V
                and play out the point

Notes:
Doubles play sequence, which brings one team (c+d) onto the defence, and the
other team (a+b) onto the offensive posture. Trainer gives both teams tactical
tips. Possible for the exercise to be played as in a match (10 points per team).

D   Doubles Training (D 8)

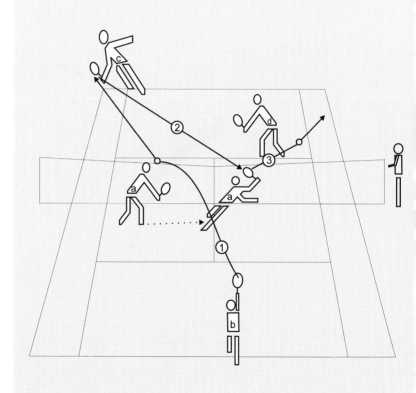

D 8   Service / Return

b: 1   = 1st (2nd) Service to c
            (followed up by service to d)
c: 2   = RETURN
            and play out the point (together with d)
a: 3   = V
            and play out the point

Aim: Coordination for deception after the service (a+b)
              Return (c+d)

Intensity: Medium-high

Time: Approx 10 minutes for each service player

Variation:
b: 1   = 1st (2nd) Service to c
c: Moves from the court centre to cover one side or the other
      (Australian line up – to the BH or FH side)
      (previous agreement with b)
      3   = V
c: 2   = RETURN
            and play out the point (together with d)

Notes:
Doubles exercise for tournament players; Players a+b communicate with sign language which deception move will be made; 2 Variations: change (1st or 2nd) service) or stay. Australian line up also possible: Player a crouches at the court centre while b serves and changes, as pre-arranged, to one or the other side.

D   Doubles Training (D 9)

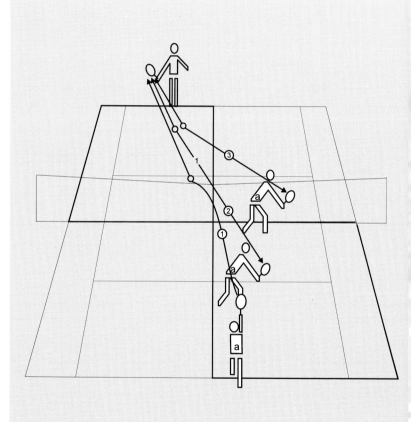

D 9 Service / Volley

T: 1 = RETURN-CR
2 + 3 = Groundstrokes (CR)
Play out the point (doubles court area)

a: 1 = 1st or 2nd Service
2 = V-CR
3 = Play out the point at the net position

Aim: Service (percentage, power-play)
Volley (mobility, leg work) as in a match,
in one half of the court (e.g., alternately up to 11 points)

Intensity: Medium-high

Time: Approx 10 minutes

1. Variation:
T: 1 = RETURN-CR and groundstrokes CR

a: 1 = Service from the advantage side
2 = V-CR
3 = Play out the point from the net position

2. Variation
T: 1 = Service
2 = V-CR
3 = Play out the point from the net position

a: 1 = RETURN-CR
2 = Groundstroke CR
3 = Play out the point

Notes:
Exercise for practice of the service/volleying (individual doubles training);
timing and mobility for the volley and smash (T may also lob), quickness of
moving forward to the net after the service; 2nd player can change places with
the trainer. Scoring as in a match (change over of service per game).

D | Doubles Training (D 10)

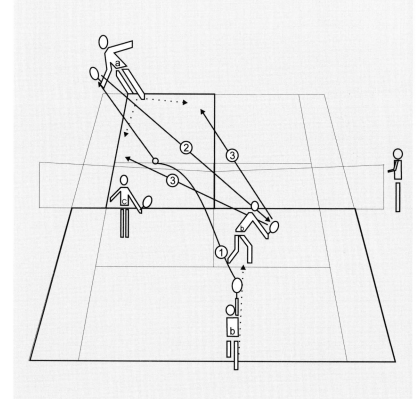

D 10   Doubles Tactics

T: Gives tactical tips

a: 2˙   = RETURN
      4   = Play out the point (one half of the doubles court)
b: 1   = 1st/2nd Service to a
      3   = V (at will) into a's single court half
             and play out the point

Aim: Doubles tactics
             on the offensive (c+b) and
             in defence (a)

Intensity: a: High
             b/c: Medium-high

Time: Approx 10 minutes per return series

Variation:
a: 2 = RETURN
      4 = Play out the point (from the advantage side) using
           only one half of the doubles court
b: 1 = 1st and 2nd service to a (advantage side)
           and play out the point (with Player c as partner)

Notes:
Exercise form, specifically for doubles, under match conditions; Players c+b in
the offensive position (covering of the net area !); Player a in the return position
(can also play lobs); change over of c/b to serve per game.

Jonathan Stark and Alex O'Brien (USA)

Mark Woodforde and Todd Woodbridge (Australia)

C   Condition Training (C 1)

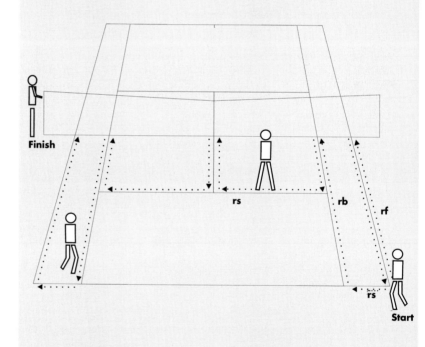

C 1 Running the Tramlines

a: Runs forwards (rf)
      Runs backwards (rb)
      Runs sidewards (rs)
b: Runs as per a but on the tramlines of the other side
c,d: Same as a,b

Aim: Speed
            Mobility

Intensity: High

Time: Approx 25-30 seconds for each series

Variation:
Hop forwards on the right leg
Hop backwards on the left leg
Side-stepping

Notes:
Carry out 2 series with suitable pauses in between. Exercise for the end of training. Trainer gives start signal, direction to be taken, and stops the time.

C Condition Training (C 2)

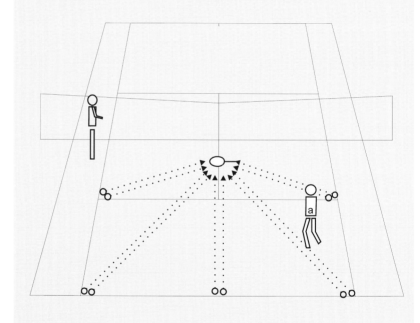

C 2 Speed

a: Collect up 6 or 8 tennis balls and place them on the racket
b: Follows Player a around

Aim: Speed
            Mobility

Intensity: High

Time: Approx 30-40 seconds

Variation:
Racket placed on the middle of the T-line
Balls (6 or 8) placed in star layout
a,b run after each other

Notes:
Change the number of tennis balls laid out. Exercise must retain a tennis cha-
racter both in form and time. Avoid anaerobic strain. Carry out cool off jogging
and stretching exercises afterwards. Trainer stops the time.

C Condition Training (C 3)

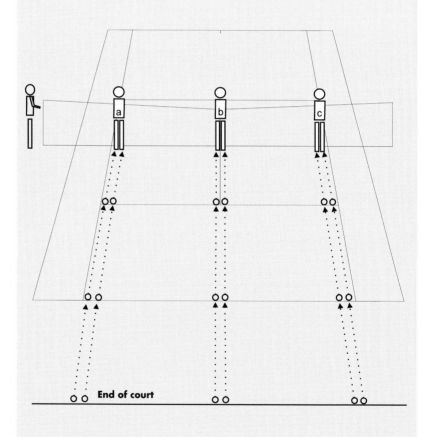

End of court

C 3 Speed

a,b,c: Collect – 2 tennis balls from the T-line
then – 2 tennis balls from the baseline
and then – 2 tennis balls from the end of tennis court/hall
then – replace the balls back in their positions

Aim: Speed
Mobility

Intensity: High

Time: Approx 40-60 seconds

Notes:
Change the number of tennis balls laid out as required. Trainer can lay down the distances to be covered. Avoid anaerobic strain. Carry out cool off jogging and stretching exercises afterwards.

C Condition Training (C 4)

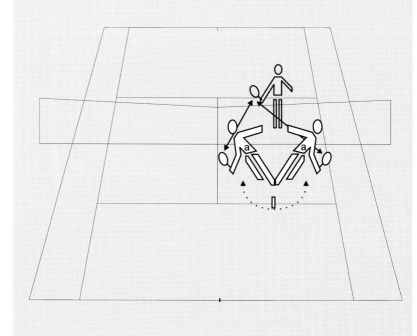

C 4 Leg Work

T: Feeds (low) from the net alternately
     Onto a's FH and BH side

a: FH-V (low) and BH-V alternately (play back to T)
b: Same as a

Aim: Speed
             Mobility

Intensity: High

Time: Approx 1-2 minutes

Variation:
T: Makes feed varied to a or b

Notes:
Exercise for the end of training. Volley should be played as low and as flat as possible from about 2-3 m distance from the net; Player a,b must flex knees while keeping the body upright. Use ball canister as marker.

Condition Training (C 5)

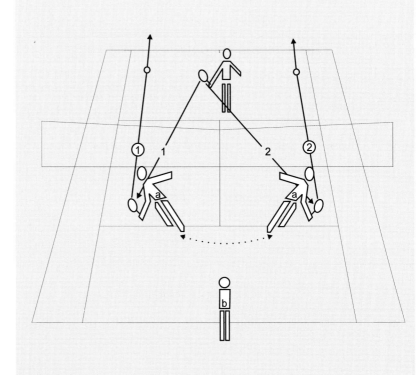

C 5 Leg work

T: Feeds onto a or b's feet
      (Alternately onto FH and BH side)

a: 1 = BH-Half-V-LL
      2 = FH-Half-V-LL
b: Same as a

Aim: Leg work
             Mobility at the net
             Reaction

Intensity: High

Time: Approx 1-2 minutes

Variation:
a: 1 = BH-Half-V-CR
      2 = FH-Half-V-CR
         (Player a decides whether he plays a volley or a half volley)

Notes:
Trainer must be capable of optimal timing for the feed (balls must bounce approx 1 m in front of the T-line); 20 balls per player is the recommended task. The half volley is also practised. Reaction training.

C Condition Training (C 6)

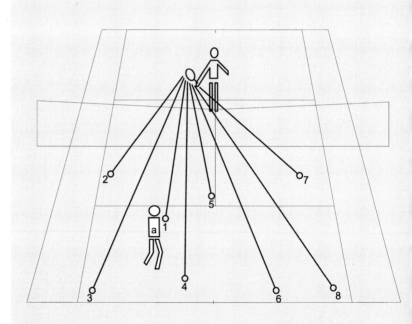

C 6 Leg work

T: Feeds 8 balls (or tosses them into play)

a: Catches each tennis ball (no racket!)
      Each ball may only bounce once
      (Balls should be dropped immediately after being caught)
b: Same as a

Aim: Leg work
            Mobility
            Speed
            Reaction

Intensity: High

Time: Approx 2 minutes (for each series of 8 tennis balls)

Variation:
a: Stands with his back to the net
      (Runs to catch the ball on T's command)

Notes:
Trainer can change the number of tennis balls. Player cannot start to run before
the ball has been fed (or tossed) by the trainer. Training for speedy reaction.
Cool off jogging and stretching exercises afterwards.

C   Condition Training (C 7)

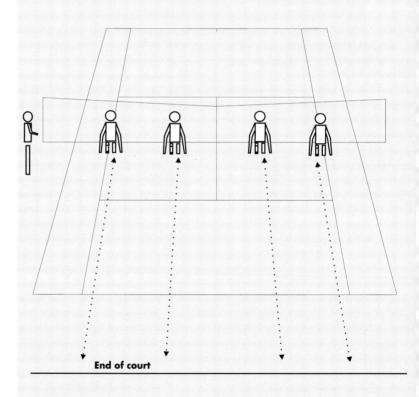

End of court

C 7 Speed

T: Calls out the commands

a,b,c,d: Sprinting from various start positions,
        Hopping one-legged,
        Walking like a duck,
        Backwards running,
        Side-stepping etc.
        to the baseline (run out to the end of the court)

Aim: Speed
        Mobility
        Reaction

Intensity: High

Time: Approx 5-10 minutes

1.   Variation:
Carry out combination of the various exercises above
carrying one or two medicine balls

2.   Variation:
Sprinting with a change of direction
at the T-line or the baseline

Notes:
Ideal closing exercise for the end of training. All players compete against each
other. Trainer must lay down a recovery rest break after each sprinting session.
Cool off jogging and stretching exercises at the end of training!

C   Condition Training (C 8)

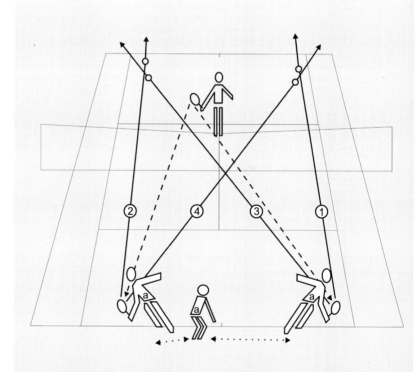

C 8 Passing Shots

T: Constant feed into a's (b's) FH and BH corner
     (T calls out the stroke direction to be played)

a: 6-8 strokes P-LL or P-CR (alternately BH and FH)
     (After each passing shot, touch the middle of the baseline)
b: Same as a

Aim: Passing shots on the run
             Leg work
             Speed

Intensity: High

Time: Approx 30 seconds per series

1.   Variation:
T: Feeds into a variety of positions

2.   Variation:
a,b: TSP-LOB or P-Short-CR (T calls which shot to play)

Notes:
Intensity must correspond to normal tennis play (6-8 passing shots); player
moves first after trainer has fed the ball. Timing of the trainer's feed is most
important. Trainer must ensure recovery rest breaks are taken.

C Condition Training (C 9)

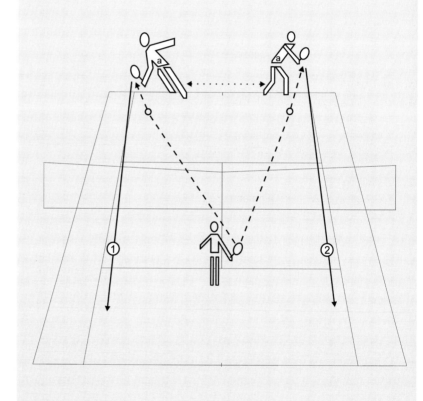

C 9 Passing Shots with Top Spin

T: Alternate feeds into a's forehand and backhand corners (from the net)

a: 1 = FH-TSP-P-LL
      2 = BH-TSP-P-LL
      etc (series of 6 or 8 passing shots)

Aim: Passing shots with top spin on the run

Intensity: High

Time: Approx 30 seconds (per series)

1.   Variation:
a: 6 or 8 passing shots played cross court only

2.   Variation:
a: 6 or 8 passing shots played TSP-LOB

3.   Variation:
a: 6 or 8 passing shots played short cross court

Notes:
Intensity must correspond to normal tennis play. Timing and rate of the trainer's feed is important. Trainer must ensure recovery rest breaks are taken.

C Condition Training (C 10)

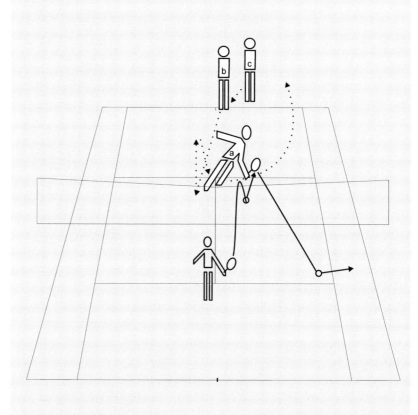

C 10   Sprinting

T: Feeds 6 balls from the net position
     (Feed onto spot about 1 m behind the net)

a: Field the 6 balls
     (The start is signified when player changes from the backwards movement
     to the forward approach, each ball must be played as a FH or BH-Volley
     before the 2nd bounce)
b: Same as a

Aim: Sprinting speed
         Leg work
         Reaction

Intensity: High

Time: Approx 30-40 seconds per series

Notes:
The start for the change of direction by the player is signified when the ball
bounces following trainer's feed. Trainer must time the feed perfectly. A full
recovery rest break (player almost regaining a steady pulse) must be taken after
each series.

C   Condition Training (C 11)

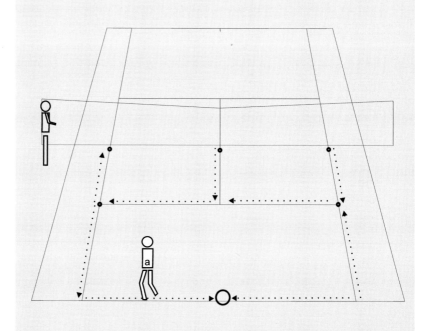

C 11   Speed

T: Gives the start signal and stops the time

a,b,c: Collect 5 tennis balls from individual points and place them down at
            the centre point of the baseline – players use the court line markings
            as running guide

Aim: Speed
            Mobility
            Leg work

Intensity: High

Time: Approx 30 seconds

Notes:
Sprint training over the distance normally experienced in a tennis match ball
exchange. Player can chose order in which he collects the balls. Each player
carries out the exercise a maximum of twice at the end of training. Ensure
recovery rest breaks are taken.

APPENDIX (BIBLIOGRAPHY)

Harre, D.: Trainingslehre, Berlin (Ost) (1971)

Heckhausen, H.: Leistungsmotivation: In: Thomae, H. (Hrsg);
    Allgemeine Psychologie 2, Motivation
    Handbuch der Psychologie Bd. 2, Göttingen (1965)

Hollmann, W. & Hettinger, T.: Sportmedizin – Arbeits- und Trainingsgrundlagen,
    Stuttgart/New York (1980)

Jonath, U.: Lexikon Trainingslehre, Reinbek (1988)

Matwejev, L.: Periodisierung des sportlichen Trainings
    Berlin/München/Frankfurt (1972)

Roethig, P.: Sportwissenschaftliches Lexikon, Schorndorf (1977)

Steinbach, M.: Psychologische Vorbereitung des Wettkampfes (1971)
    In: Carl K, Psychologie im Training und Wettkampf Berlin (1973)

Weber, K.: Tennis-Fitness, München/Wien/Zürich (1982)

ABOUT THE AUTHOR

Lutz Steinhöfel
- Born 1956 in Berlin
- Graduate Sports Teacher
- Studied at the German Sports Academy in Cologne

Sports Career:

1974 and 1975
- International participation and representation for the German Tennis Federation (Valerio and Galea Cup)

1975 - 1986
- German Tennis League (Bundesliga) player for:
  Rochus Club Düsseldorf (1976)
  HTC Blau Weiss Krefeld (1977-1979)
  Blau Weiss Neuss (1980-1985)
  RTHC Bayer Leverkusen (1986)

1983 - 1985
- Three times German Champion with Blau Weiss Neuss (at position 5 or 6)

1986 - 1991
- Sports Director, Head Coach and Trainer of the German Tennis League (Bundesliga) Team RTHC Bayer Leverkusen

1985 - 1992
- Instructor for the speciality of tennis at the German Sports Academy Cologne

since 1992
- Head Coach and Trainer of the German Tennis League (Bundesliga) Team Blau Weiss Neuss

1992 and 1994
- German Champion with Blau Weiss Neuss

1993
- German Champion (Over 35's)

Further sporting highlights:

5-times Champion of the Lower Rhine Federation Mens-Singles Tournament (1977, 1978, 1979, 1980 and 1982)
Named "Mr Bundesliga" 1983 (unbeaten in 12 German Tennis League (Bundesliga) matches during the 1983 German Tennis League season
Highest ranking in the National German Men's listing - 14th